DREAM AGAIN - Is God Calling You to More?

Awaken lost dreams, discover new ones, and step into your divine destiny

Judy Rushfeldt

ISBN-13: 9781894375030

Printed in Canada

CONTENTS

ENDORSEMENTS

Cheryl Weber, Host of "100 Huntley Street"

"Dream Again is a powerful reminder that fear, disappointment, or delay never disqualify God's purpose for your life. With heartfelt honesty and practical wisdom, Judy Rushfeldt offers more than encouragement—she gives you a step-by-step path to healing, clarity, and renewed vision. If your dreams have been buried under the weight of life's setbacks, this book will help you rise, refocus, and move forward with bold, unshakable faith."

Drs. George & Hazel Hill, President and Founders, Victory Churches International

"We highly recommend this excellent book by Judy Rushfeldt which will equip you to find and live out your God-given destiny. Step by step the path laid out by God, before you were born, begins to unfold, and the excitement begins to build as your future becomes clear. You will learn how your gifts, passions, and life experiences blend together to lead you to your unique calling. Just as important, you will learn how to push through fears, self-doubt, and opposition to fulfill the unique purpose that God has for you."

Margaret Gibb, Founder & Executive Director, Women Together

"Award-winning author Judy Rushfeldt has once again dipped into her deep well of experience and knowledge to write *Dream Again: Is God Calling You to More.*

This book is perfect for those who have lost their ability to visualize their future. It provides powerful answers to those daunting questions that too often destroy our will to dream. Filled with practical instructions for discerning a calling and overcoming the obstacles and fears that every leader faces, *Dream Again* makes for life-empowering reading."

Carson Pue, Executive Mentor, Leadership Coach, and Best-Selling Author of *Mentoring Leaders* and *Lead Like a Saint.*

"*Dream Again* is both inspiration and a roadmap for anyone seeking God's purpose. With warmth and wisdom, Judy Rushfeldt blends practical tools and spiritual insight to help you turn gifts—and even pain—into a life aligned with God's biggest dreams for you. If you're longing for clarity around your calling, walking through hard seasons, or simply desiring to live with deeper purpose, this book will be a faithful companion on your journey."

Carol Kent, Founder & Executive Director of Speak Up Ministries, Best-selling author of *When I Lay My Isaac Down* and *He Holds My Hand*

"Judy Rushfeldt has crafted an extraordinarily practical and uplifting guide for every Christian who has felt their dreams slip away in recent years. With warmth and biblical wisdom, *Dream Again* walks you through the process of releasing past disappointments, recognizing God's voice, and taking concrete steps toward the unique purpose He has designed for you. This well-written book provides actionable strategies to overcome fear, write your mission statement, and become the hands and feet of Christ in a hurting world. Prepare to awaken dreams you thought were dead and discover that with God, all things are still possible."

Dr. Jennifer McVety, Vice-President & Academic Registrar, Canada Christian College

"This book provides a biblical remedy for restoring dreams. Even in the midst of trials and tribulations, this promise of hope persists, guaranteeing that He will do exceedingly abundantly above and beyond all that we ask. This book offers insightful wisdom, biblical teaching, and practical application from our accomplished author. Through this writing, your dreams can be revived, and life can be lived more abundantly."

Pastor Dave Meyers, Vice-President of Victory Churches of Canada

"Reading the book *Dream Again* was a powerful reminder to me that it's never too late, and we're never so far, to see our life's vision, purpose, and dreams live again. This book is filled scriptural principles, inspiring stories, practical wisdom, and hands-on tools that will help you discover, dust off, and place your dreams back on track. If you think it's simply too late, or life's just been too hard to see your dreams come back to life, then *Dream Again* is the book for you."

INTRODUCTION

Global pandemics. Lockdowns. Loss of loved ones. International conflicts. Moral collapse. Persecution. Social chaos.

The past several years have taken a toll and eroded the faith of many Christians in God's sovereignty, power, purpose, and provision. Disappointments, delays, and disruptions have left many paralyzed by doubt, anxiety, and uncertainty—hesitant to take new steps of faith or to believe God for greater things.

For some, it feels as though a part of them has died —the part that once loved to step out courageously and believe God for big dreams. When the fulfillment of God-given desires seems delayed or derailed, our hopes and potential can slowly become buried beneath coffins of fear and regret. The sad reality is that many of God's children have allowed their dreams to die.

Yet while the world has changed—and continues to change at a dizzying pace—one thing remains constant: the unshakable promise of Jesus, "With men this is impossible, but with God all things are possible" (Mat. 19:26).

Dream Again – Is God Calling You to More? is an invitation to release past disappointments, awaken dormant dreams, and trust God for new ones. It is about moving forward with fresh courage, daring to believe that His purpose for your life is bigger than your setbacks, and embracing the adventure of walking with Him into more.

God has entrusted you with a unique blend of gifts, skills, passions, and personality. They are God's investment in you – intended to bless others and advance His kingdom. When you discover and steward them faithfully, you step into the joy of living aligned with your divine design. The question is not whether your life will make a difference, but what kind of difference it will make.

The same Spirit who gave you your gifts also promises to empower you to use them. Every day is an opportunity to invest what He has placed in your hands—for His glory and the good of others.

In the pages ahead, you will discover how to:

- Discern God's voice and leading
- Discover or re-discover your passions and gifts
- Clarify and write your mission statement, vision statement, and action plan
- Face obstacles and trials with courage, knowing God uses them to shape your character and prepare you for greater influence
- Use what is already in your hand, trusting God to multiply its impact far beyond what you imagine.

It's time to dream again – not with shallow wishful thinking, but with Spirit-led faith. Starting today, dare to believe Him for more—and prepare to be amazed at what He will do in and through your life.

Dedicated to the One who gives life, dreams, and purpose

Now to him who is able to do immeasurably more than all we ask or imagine, according to his power that is at work within us, to him be glory in the church and in Christ Jesus throughout all generations, for ever and ever! – Eph. 3:19-20 NIV

WAIT -- BEFORE YOU GET STARTED

Chapters 9 and 10 of DREAM AGAIN are about mission and vision statements. You will learn about the benefits and characteristics of effective mission and vision statements, and will be provided with several examples.

If you would like more detailed information about how to write mission and vision statements, I would love to send you my free e-book, entitled *Write Your Personal Mission and Vision Statements.* This guide includes much more information than I have space to provide in this book.

To get your free guide today, go to: JudyRushfeldt.com

PART I: DREAM

With men, this is impossible, but with God, all things are possible – Jesus

CHAPTER ONE
DREAM AGAIN

Growing up, I was far more interested in Superman and Wonder Woman than princess stories or Barbie dolls. I was introduced to the world of superheroes through comic books like Batman and Supergirl; children's literature and fairy tales with heroes and heroines like Gretel who rescued her brother Hansel from the wicked witch; and Peter, Susan, Edmund, and Lucy who together with Aslan the lion saved Narnia from the cruel witch and her evil armies.

I loved stories of good conquering evil, justice prevailing over injustice, and courageous heroes and heroines risking their lives to defend the innocent.

So, it's no surprise that as a teenager, I was attracted to the *Mission Impossible* TV series, which was later developed into a movie series.

If you have ever watched a *Mission Impossible* movie,

you'll know that Ethan Hunt (played by Tom Cruise) is characterized as a true-blue hero with a noble moral compass. Every movie has been a resounding success, which *Forbes Magazine* attributes to Hunt's courage and integrity.

"Its popularity is a testament to the power of a hero who is unquestionably good, who will never sacrifice innocent people," wrote Scott Mendelson in *Forbes Magazine*. "There is just as much artistic value, if not more so in these grim, dark times, in the notion of a hero stopping the bad guys without becoming a bad guy, and who shows the rest of the dark world that his decency is not a weakness, but rather his greatest strength."[1]

Every movie starts with Ethan Hunt listening to an audio recording. The anonymous recorded voice says, "Your mission, should you choose to accept it, is..." And then the mysterious spymaster describes some wild and dangerous assignment, with little chance of survival or success. At the end the voice says, "This tape will self-destruct in five seconds."

Ethan Hunt never failed to accept the mission, and together with his loyal team he always succeeded against impossible odds, saving the world from nuclear war, mass terrorism, or some other global disaster.

Do you have a mission? Have you accepted it? Most important, are you living it?

Unlike Ethan Hunt in *Mission Impossible*, most of us are not called to fight literal criminals and terrorists (although some are). Our mission involves standing against the spiritual forces of darkness and expanding the kingdom of God in our areas of influence.

I love this Bible verse: "They that know their God, shall be strong, and do great exploits." [2]

The term *exploit* is defined as a heroic act; a deed of renown; a noble achievement. It is typically understood to include opposition, risk, and sometimes, danger.

That's what many Bible heroes and heroines of faith experienced as they chose to accept the unique mission that God had for each one of them.

And like the biblical men and women of faith, God has called each one of us to know Him, become strong in Him, and fulfill a kingdom mission for Him. At times, it will involve risk, opposition, and suffering. But in the end, it will be worth it.

It's Time for More

Global pandemics. Lockdowns. Loss of loved ones. Wars. Division. Moral depravity. Persecution. Social chaos. Financial loss.

The past several years have taken their toll. When lockdowns ended after the Covid-19 pandemic, the psychologists, cultural anthropologists, and political pundits predicted life would go back to normal.

They were wrong. Several years later, many people are still suffering from poor mental health, fear of the future, and anxiety about the economy, political upheaval, climate disasters, and international conflicts.

For many Christians, there has also been an erosion of faith in God's sovereignty, power, purpose, and provision. The chaos, loss, and disappointments have caused many to feel paralyzed by doubt, constrained from taking new steps of faith and believing God for big things.

I call it a *lockdown of the heart.*

You may feel like a part of you has died– the part of you that believed God for big dreams, that loved to step out in faith and was passionate about believing Him for greater purpose and destiny. When there has been a delay in seeing the fulfillment of what we believe God has called us to do, for whatever reason, over time our hopes, dreams, and potential can become buried in coffins of doubt, fear, and timidity.

The sad reality is that many of God's children have allowed their dreams to die. Others have shrunk them to a size that can be easily managed and achieved with human effort, rather than believing God for big dreams that can only come to pass through His grace and power.

But while the world has changed, and continues to change at a rapid pace, one thing that will never change is Jesus' promise, "With men this is impossible, but with God all things are possible." [3]

My friends, it's time to dream again.

It's time to break up the fallow ground – the places in our hearts that have become numb and hardened from disappointments, delays, and uncertainty. It's time to lift our hearts and spiritual eyes to the King of Kings, the Lord of Lords, and to once again believe His promise that with God, all things are possible.

There is nothing in your life: not your past mistakes, failures, sins or hurts; not the problems and obstacles you're encountering right now; not other people; and not any evil or spiritual opposition, that can stand in the way of God's love for you and His purpose for your life.

Forget the Past

A crucial pre-requisite to stepping into more of God's purpose is to shift our focus away from what has not happened, or what has happened that eroded our trust in God and begin to dream again. God spoke through the prophet Isaiah:

Thus says the Lord, who makes a way in the sea,
And a path through the mighty waters,
"Do not remember the former things,
Nor consider the things of old.
Behold, I will do a new thing, Now it shall spring forth;
Shall you not know it?
I will even make a road in the wilderness.
And rivers in the desert."[4]

Shall you not know it? The amplified translation of that verse reads: *"Now it springs forth; Do you not perceive and know it and will you not give heed to it?"*

Why would God ask this question? It suggests to me that it is possible to become blinded to the new things that God wants to birth in and through our lives if we keep looking backwards and remain stuck, fearful, or unwilling to take new steps of faith.

God's message is clear. "I have something new for you. Will you let go of the past? Will you release the disappointments, pain, and regrets of the previous season, and look to the future? Will you choose to take the next step on the pathway of purpose I designed just for you?"

Paul the apostle also emphasized the need to forget the past and look to the future:

> *I press on, that I may lay hold of that for which Christ Jesus has also laid hold of me. Brethren, I do not count myself to have apprehended; but one thing I do, forgetting those things which are behind and reaching forward to those things which are ahead, I press toward the goal for the prize of the upward call of God in Christ Jesus.*[5]

The time is now to free our imagination and creativity from the prisons of doubt and fear and learn to dream again.

After all, God created us in His image. And among His many wonderful and majestic characteristics, He is a dreamer – an extravagantly creative dreamer. Why else would He create 10,000 species of frogs including Titicaca frogs, chocolate frogs, scrotum frogs, pig frogs, Pacific tree frogs, water frogs, mountain chicken frogs, Ba Ba frogs, Panamanian Golden frogs, and more?

Why would He create 250,000 species of flowers? It's not like we need flowers that reflect every possible pattern, shape, texture, and colour to support the ecosystem. God did not create things for mere functionality. He loves beauty and colour and creativity – all of nature sings of His extravagance and splendor. The diversity of creation never fails to amaze me.

If the natural environment portrays His creativity and beauty, how much more do you and I have the potential to express His diversity, creativity, and beauty? After all, the Bible tells us that human beings are the crown of God's creation, the pinnacle of His creativity.

What does that mean for you and me? If God is a creative visionary and we are progressively being conformed into His image through our relationship with

Christ, it means each one of us is endowed with the ability to envision, imagine, and dream.

God did not create us to live a small, safe life. He did not create us for mediocrity. He created us for the extraordinary. For a destiny. And He has given us everything we need to fulfill that destiny.

Not only do we have the ability to dream, we *need* to dream. Did you know that with no vision of purpose, we hinder our spiritual growth? Without a clear sense of purpose, our spiritual growth loses direction and momentum. We risk forgetting our need for God's guidance and intervention. Our hearts may grow content in self-reliance, leaving little room for divine dependence. It's only when we take bold steps of faith that we truly encounter the fullness of His supernatural power.

Why? God's power is for a purpose. It's not meant to help us *feel* powerful, or to pursue a selfish agenda, or to boast, show off our gifts, or control and manipulate others. God's divine power is intended to fulfill a unique purpose that will expand His kingdom and bless others. But it is not activated unless we draw on it. And if we rarely step out in faith, there's no demand or draw, thus no power.

It's similar to an electrical outlet in your home. You can plug major appliances into the outlet that require more power, like your TV, microwave, air conditioner, and washing machine. You can also plug small items into it that need very little power, like a nightlight or electric toothbrush. The amount of power that is released through the electrical outlet depends solely on what demand is placed on it.

Is your dream big enough to require a large infusion of God's grace and power?

Pursuing a God-sized vision will ignite your prayer life like nothing else. Do you have little goals that don't require much of God's power? Or do you have big dreams that will never come to pass without Him, that drive you to your knees in prayer and utter dependence on the Holy Spirit? God longs for us to live by faith, because He wants to do marvelous things in and through us.

As the writer of Hebrews said,

> *Without faith it is impossible to please Him, for he who comes to God must believe that He is, and that He is a rewarder of those who diligently seek Him.*[6]

Do you have a dream that burns in your heart, a dream that is stretching your faith, igniting your prayer life, and motivating you to do things that you know you cannot do on your own?

Jesus said we need to become like little children in our relationship with Him, trusting Him with the simplicity of a child. Remember when you were a child? For most children, at least those raised in a stable environment, it was easy to dream.

There were no boundaries to our imagination, no limits to the possibilities, no inner critic to tell us all the reasons why we will never find the pot at the end of the rainbow. Our hearts were open, soft, and full of wonder. Our magical brains saw the world as an endless display of possibilities and potential. For a child, the possibilities are endless.

But somewhere along the journey of growing up,

most of us reframed our dreams. We shrunk them to a size that was safe, secure, and manageable. Conformity and predictability took the place of adventure and risk. Comfort and security became more important than calling and destiny.

We succumbed to the lie that tells us we are not enough. Or that the obstacles are insurmountable. Or that we will never succeed.

Do you feel as though you are too old? Too young? Too broken, too timid, too ordinary? That you are simply not enough? Not smart enough, gifted enough, rich enough, talented enough, pretty or handsome enough?

Did someone steal your dream through criticism, mockery, or betrayal? Did you take steps toward a dream, but gave up after you were bombarded with an endless litany of disappointments, delays, and setbacks?

One of the most common dream killers is delay – lengthy and seemingly meaningless delays. Delays especially challenge our faith when they also involve adversity and loss.

But delays and adversity are all part of God growing our faith and character. Every Bible hero and heroine endured setbacks, adversity, and lengthy delays before they experienced the fulfillment of God's call and promises. Why? Because God was building their character and faith so He could do greater things through their lives. And faith champions are not built in a life of perpetual ease and comfort.

Abraham and Sarah waited twenty-five years before the Lord gave them Isaac, years that severely tested their faith. David waited some fifteen years after Samuel anointed him as king before he actually ascended to the throne, and he had to overcome many obstacles and attacks before that promise was realized. Joseph endured thirteen years in slavery and prison before God fulfilled his dream. Hannah waited through nineteen years of barrenness and public reproach before the Lord finally fulfilled her dream of having a child.

Moses, Joshua, and Caleb waited over forty years in the wilderness before they saw the promised land – years of trials, tests, and disappointment.

However, while all of them were waiting, they were not passive in their waiting. They continued to trust and obey God amid disappointment and adversity. And through it all, God tested and grew their faith and character. That's all part of becoming a champion of faith.

In every one of their lives, when their moment of opportunity finally came, they were prepared. They were ready to step boldly into the greater calling God had for them.

My friends, it's time to dream again. It's time to let go of all the disappointments of the past season and look to your Heavenly Father for the new things that He would love to birth in and through your life. He is calling you to greater purpose, vision, and fruitfulness.

Whatever your situation, God has called you to more.

God has a Dream, and He needs you to fulfil it

God not only wants you to dream – He *needs* you to dream. That's because God has a dream, and He can only fulfill it through you and me.

What is God's dream? What are the desires of His

heart? What are the dreams that burn so passionately in His heart that He was willing to endure agonizing pain, torture, and death?

One clue to answering that question is to ask, *What breaks God's heart?* The Bible tells us that sin breaks His heart, because of how it separates people from Him. Injustice, abuse, and discrimination break His heart. Physical, emotional, and mental pain and illness break His heart. Suffering children break his heart. Sexual slavery breaks His heart. Human trafficking breaks His heart. Lonely seniors break His heart. Drug-addicted teenagers break His heart. Abandoned orphans break His heart. Moral depravity breaks His heart. Poverty breaks His heart. Most of all, His lost sons and daughters break His heart.

And what is God's dream? He dreams of redeeming hurting humanity. He dreams of every person on this planet receiving the gift of salvation and eternal life. He dreams of delivering every single person from the bondage of sin, Satan, and spiritual blindness. He dreams of rescuing children from abuse, poverty, and sexual slavery. He dreams of healing broken hearts and lives, of breaking chains of pain and despair, and releasing every person into their destiny as His precious sons and daughters. He dreams of every man, woman, and child spending eternity with Him.

And the unique purpose God has planned for you is all about giving Him the desire of His heart, so He can fulfill *His* big dream.

Jesus made several statements about His purpose, including:

I have come that they may have life, and that they may have it more abundantly.[7]

I have come into the world as a light, so that no one who believes in me should stay in darkness.[8]

For I have come down from heaven not to do my will but to do the will of him who sent me.[9]

For even the Son of Man did not come to be served, but to serve, and to give His life a ransom for many. [10]

For the Son of Man has come to seek and to save that which was lost.[11]

My favourite passage is found in Luke chapter four, where He said:

"The Spirit of the Lord is upon Me,
Because He has anointed Me
To preach the gospel to the poor;
He has sent Me to heal the broken-hearted,
To proclaim liberty to the captives
And recovery of sight to the blind,
To set at liberty those who are oppressed;
To proclaim the acceptable year of the Lord. [12]

There you have it: God's dream in a nutshell. It's a big dream, an amazing dream, a beautiful dream.

How will God fulfill His dream? Through you and me. That means that we must live divine dreams. How else can we be His hands and feet and voice to reach out with love to a lost and hurting world?

Ultimately, stepping into your divine purpose is not about you. It's not about me. It's about Father God's desires and dreams. And as each of us chooses to move forward on our personal pathway of purpose, we can be more effective in helping God fulfill His dreams. And while ultimately it is not about you or me, we are blessed when we accept God's invitation to partner with Him in expanding the kingdom of Christ on earth. What joy! What a privilege!

Perhaps you have already reached a dream. If so, Jesus wants to give you a new one. God did not create you to stagnate. You may have invested a lot of time, effort, and resources in that dream. But it's time to move on. It's time to follow Jesus' call to new horizons of destiny and purpose.

God has called us to dream, live the dream, then dream again.

If your dream has died, and it's God's dream for you, Jesus wants to breathe new life into it. If someone or something stole your dream, He wants to redeem it. If fear, self-doubt, or criticism have buried your dream, He wants to resurrect it.

Whatever your situation, God has called you to become more, dream more, and do more. He is calling you to greater vision, purpose, and effectiveness.

> *For we are His workmanship [His own master work, a work of art], created in Christ Jesus [reborn from above —spiritually transformed, renewed, ready to be used] for good works, which God prepared [for us] beforehand [taking paths which He set], so that we would walk in them.*[13]

Jesus is inviting you to live the life you were always meant to live. He is calling you to become the man or woman that He had in mind when He formed you in your mother's womb. He is challenging you to do the things He created, wired, and destined you to do.

Are you up to the challenge? Are you open to the Holy Spirit waking the divine dreams He has placed in you? Are you willing for Him to lead you on paths you have never walked before? Are you willing to climb out of your rut, step out of your comfort zone, and allow God to expand and enlarge your vision to embrace new dimensions of purpose that He has designed just for you? Are you ready to join Him on a new adventure of faith?

My friends, it's time to dream again.

I'm a little pencil in the hand of a writing God,
who is sending a love letter to
the world —Mother Teresa

CHAPTER TWO

WHAT IS DIVINE MISSION?

"The two most important days in your life are the day you are born and the day you find out why," wrote Mark Twain, an author who many refer to as the father of American literature.

Finding your *why* starts with asking "What is mission?" For a child of God, mission is your divine purpose or calling. (Throughout this book, I use the terms *mission, purpose,* and *calling* interchangeably).

The same God who designed the splendors of the universe personally planned every little detail about you, including your physical characteristics, personality, talents, and, most important—your life purpose. He never planned for you to live a trivial, meaningless life. He designed you for a purpose that will make an eternal impact in your sphere of influence.

Divine purpose is not something you choose; it is something you discover. And the discovery process is a journey. I call it the *pathway of purpose*; how far you progress on that path is up to you. It reflects the choices you make along the way in developing your relationship with God, allowing Him to mature your character, and stewarding the gifts, assignments, and opportunities He entrusts to you.

For the remainder of this chapter, we will look at some of the most important characteristics of divine purpose.

Purpose is Redemptive

For you created my inmost being; you knit me together in my mother's womb. I praise you because I am fearfully and wonderfully made; your works are wonderful, I know that full well. Your eyes saw my unformed body; all the days ordained for me were written in your book before one of them came to be.[14]

If God ordained all our days as David wrote in this psalm, what about all the bad things that happen to us? What about the tragedies, sickness, abuse, failures, and sins? Did God plan all that?

No, God did not plan those things. The Bible affirms that God's plans for us are good. But the reality is that we are born into a fallen world. God's divine purposes can be thwarted and delayed by sin, by our own choices, by Satan, and by the choices of others who harm us. Also, His purposes can be hindered by the tragedy and pain that are a consequence of living in a fallen world.

But that is not the end of the story. It is merely the context for history's most beautiful story—the victorious message that Jesus Christ paid the price for us to be set free from the repercussions of our sin and bad choices, as well as the wounds and brokenness resulting from other people's sins against us.

As everyone knows, bad things happen to good people, including Christians who are serving God with all their hearts. But while God did not plan those things, He did plan how He would bring good out of evil and restore purpose out of brokenness.

> *And we know that all things work together for good to those who love God, to those who are called according to His purpose.*[15]

All things. The good things, the confusing things, the painful things. The things we understand, and the things that will never make sense this side of heaven. If we trust Him, God will bring good out of every disappointment, failure, heartache, and tragedy.

One of the words the Bible frequently uses to describe Jesus Christ is *Redeemer*. The Bible is rich with promises of redemption through Jesus Christ.

What is redemption? The original Greek and Hebrew words from which the terms *redeem* and *redemption* are translated mean "to buy back." In biblical times, these terms described the cultural practice of paying a full ransom to free a slave or to gain back property that had been taken.

As our Redeemer, Jesus paid the price with his own life to set us free from slavery to inner prisons of sin and brokenness. Not only that, He also paid the price to redeem lost property; that property represents the promises of scripture as well as God's unique call upon your life.

Though God cannot change your past, he can create beauty and purpose from the ashes of sin, disappointment, tragedy, and failure.

I call this *redemptive purpose*. Redemptive purpose is the miracle by which God integrates all of life's experiences into something good – something with the potential to bless us and other people through us. It is the miracle by which God can take the shattered dreams, disappointments, regrets, dumb choices, and broken areas of our lives and create a masterpiece of beauty.

Our heavenly Father takes our greatest weaknesses, deepest pains, and darkest shame; applies his healing oil, binds up our wounds, and redeems the wonderful purpose he has cherished in His heart since before we were born.

The very thing you consider your greatest handicap may one day become a key to unlocking your greatest potential. Often it is at the point of our most debilitating weakness that God's power is most beautifully demonstrated. As Jesus said to the apostle Paul, "My grace if sufficient for you, for My strength is made perfect in weakness."[16]

Take best-selling author Christian Caine, for example. Between the ages of three and twelve she suffered repeated sexual abuse from several men. Yet she overcame a childhood of sexual abuse to become a fearless crusader for Christ in the fight against human trafficking. Together with her husband Nick, she founded the anti-human trafficking organization, *The A21 Campaign;* they received the Mother Theresa Memorial award for their work combating human trafficking among refugees.

In an interview published on Propel Women, Christine said, "Through the work of A21, God has taken the shame I carried of abuse, adoption, and abandonment, and is redeeming it for trafficked victims from all over the world!" [17]

She said that the very things that you think have disqualified you are often the ones that in fact qualify you to do what God has called you to do. "Anything meant in this world for evil, God can use for good. God is able to take the mess of our past and turn it into a message. He takes our trials and tests and turns them into a testimony." [18]

I love Christine's story, for it paints a beautiful portrait of God's power to create beauty from the ashes of pain, regrets, and disappointments. Our Father specializes in restoring dormant purpose and resurrecting dead dreams. He is committed to liberating us to become the person He had in mind when He created us, leading us into a wonderful inheritance as His son or daughter.

Divine Purpose is Irrevocable

God's calling for your life never changes. Paul the apostle wrote, "For the gifts and calling of God are irrevocable." [19] *Irrevocable* means: unable to be repealed or annulled; unalterable. While the context of this verse refers to God's promises to the Jewish people, many other Bible verses affirm that God is faithful to fulfill His promises.

We have a part to play, however. Many of God's promises require action on our part before they are fulfilled. For example, the Bible promises that if we confess our sins, God is faithful and just to forgive our sins. But if we refuse to confess, we cannot expect forgiveness to automatically take place. As another example, Jesus tells us that if we refuse to forgive others, God will not forgive us.

Some people feel that they are too messed up for God to work through them. Others feel they have wasted too much time, or committed too many sins, or resisted God for too many years. That is simply not true. Other people, circumstances, tragedies, and even your own failures and bad choices can never destroy God's dream for your life! Divine purpose is indestructible.

You can be ninety years old, but still make your remaining years count for eternity. After all, Jesus' ministry only lasted three years. It's never too late to develop the gifts and potential God has placed in you. It's never too late to begin again. God's mercies are new every morning. Decide that starting today, you will commit yourself to discovering and fulfilling your purpose.

Divine Purpose is Unique

I like to describe divine purpose as *spiritual DNA*. In the same way that God wove together your physical genetic blueprint while you were still in your mother's womb, He designed your spiritual DNA. Scientists will never see this under a microscope. But it's no less real.

Your purpose is as unique as you. God designed you to meet a need that nobody else can meet quite like you. Just as your physical genetic code is unique, so is your spiritual DNA.

You may have similar talents, gifts, or vision as someone else, but they will manifest differently through your unique personality, life message, experiences, and passions.

In later chapters, we will expand on the uniqueness of your calling.

Divine Purpose must be Nurtured

While divine purpose is indestructible, it can remain dormant. There are many reasons for this. One is a lack of knowledge. Many people simply don't realize that God has a special purpose for their lives.

Others never reach their potential because they try to do it independently of God. Since God made you, it's impossible to truly know your potential or fulfill your purpose outside of a relationship with him.

Another reason many people never discover or fulfill their purpose is because of inner brokenness. Having been afflicted by tragedy, rejection, abuse, or other trauma, they find it difficult to believe in a loving and faithful God. Still others are bound by fears, doubts, feelings of inadequacy, and cynicism.

Some people don't nurture divine purpose because they have given up, having succumbed to doubt and discouragement after years of adversity, delays, and seemingly unanswered prayers.

To mature and grow, divine purpose requires the right spiritual environment.

The first and most important step to creating the right spiritual environment is have a personal relationship with God through Jesus Christ. Through Christ, we receive the grace and power to become the person God created us to be, and to do the things He has called us to do.

Jesus said, "You must be born again."[20] At the time, He was having a conversation with a man named Nicodemus, a Jewish ruler who visited Jesus one night with questions about His teachings. Nicodemus asked, "How can a man be born when he is old?"

Jesus responded, "Most assuredly, I say to you, unless one is born of water and the Spirit, he cannot enter the kingdom of God. That which is born of the flesh is flesh, and that which is born of the Spirit is spirit." [21]

Jesus was referring to spiritual birth. What did He mean? It's simple – we are spiritually born when we make the choice to believe that Jesus died to pay the price for our sins, that He rose again, then ask His forgiveness and invite Him to be our Savior and Lord. You cannot earn it, work for it, or become good enough for it. None of us are good enough. It's a free gift. But like any gift, you must receive it to benefit from it.

When we are born again, our spirit is awakened to God. Rather than just knowing about God or believing in the existence of God, we truly *know* Him in our newly born spirit, for God's presence indwells us.

Through relationship with Christ, His Spirit empowers you to become the person He created you to be and fulfill the potential He placed inside of you. With the power of God working in you, previously dormant seeds of purpose and potential are germinated by what Jesus called "living waters" – the Holy Spirit.

But we must do our part to water and fertilize those seeds for them to mature and blossom into the fulness of divine potential and purpose.

My husband, Brian, plants a vegetable garden every

spring – typically carrots, spinach, zucchini, beets, lettuce, and broccoli. One year, he misplaced a package of carrot seeds in a drawer and forgot about it. Two years later, he discovered the misplaced package. The seeds looked the same of course. And despite sitting dormant in a drawer for two years, once he planted the seeds, they germinated, grew, and eventually produced sweet tasting carrots.

In a similar manner, if we do not plant the seeds of purpose in the right spiritual environment, they never mature. They never reach their potential. But there's good news: they never die. The moment we commit ourselves to nurturing the seeds of purpose, God infuses His power and grace into those seeds and causes them to germinate, grow, and over time blossom into the beautiful purpose God intended.

Through Christ, we receive the grace and power to become the person God created us to be, and to do the things He has called us to do.

Right up until the moment you breathe your last breath, the seeds of divine purpose remain in your heart, waiting for the right spiritual environment to germinate and grow. Regardless of how old you are, how many mistakes you have made, how far you have strayed from God, or how many years you have neglected your gifts and talents—it is never too late.

It is up to you to believe, receive, and apply His grace and power. Purpose does not automatically unfold. God is the author of divine purpose, but each of us plays a vital part in whether or not that purpose is realized.

Purpose is not Fame

Sometimes, we get the idea that divine purpose must involve grandiose ideas and achievements, like winning a Nobel prize, finding a cure for cancer, or evangelizing entire nations. We think of great inventions, famous authors, world evangelists, composers, and speakers. In comparison, we think: *My gifts and talents are so insignificant compared to them.*

I like something Dr. Martin Luther King Jr. said, "Everyone has the power for greatness—not for fame but greatness, because greatness is determined by service."

God doesn't measure success in terms of fame, numbers, or popularity. Success, in God's eyes, is obedience to His word and revealed will. If you focus on fulfilling God will and purpose for you, you will be successful in His eyes. And you will have an impact for eternity.

God has called you to run *your* race. Not the race of others you admire. Not the race other people think you should run. Your race. God will equip and empower you to run your race, but He will not empower you to run someone else's race.

No doubt you have heard of Winston Churchill. Countless books have been written about him;, many documentaries have been produced, and he is quoted in many books and speeches. After all, he not only saved his own nation, but he saved the entire free world from being taken over by a dangerous and repressive Nazi regime. He was far from perfect of course. But were it not for his moral courage, leadership, boldness, and relentless tenacity, we would all be living under a Nazi dictatorship today. We would not have any of the freedoms we enjoy and take for granted.

There is another name that you have likely *not* heard before: Elizabeth Anne Everest. After all, Elizabeth Everest was never a leader in politics, society, or ministry. She never wrote a book or gave a speech or led a nation. What did she do? She was a nanny.

But for Elizabeth Anne Everest, serving as a nanny was not merely a job; it was a ministry. A powerful, fearless Christian, she lived her faith boldly and worked hard to build godliness and biblical truth into the young lives in her care.

And so it came to be that in February of 1875, God entrusted Elizabeth Anne Everest to become the live-in nanny and primary influence in the life of a baby boy by the name of Winston Leonard Spencer Churchill.

For all intents and purposes, she was also Winston's surrogate mother and father. Winston's parents were active in society but emotionally distant and neglectful. Although many British Victorian parents had little to do with raising their children, the Churchills were distant even by Victorian standards. Historians say that Winston's father thought his son was mentally disabled. He rarely talked to Winston and regularly vented his mounting rage on the child. More than one historian has concluded that Lord Randolph simply despised his son.

Elizabeth Everest was the one who loved and comforted young Winston. She was the one who wiped away his tears and tucked him in at night. And it was with his beloved nanny that young Winston first experienced genuine Christianity. He would see her praying silently and ask her about it. On bended knee beside this gentle woman of God he first learned about prayer and heard the scriptures. Everest sang hymns with him and had long talks about Jesus and eternal life. She boldly counseled him about ethics, values, and scripture; she trained him to develop virtues of courage, honesty, sacrifice, and perseverance.

In *Never Give In: The Extraordinary Character of Winston Churchill,* author Stephen Mansfield describes Everest's influence on young Winston.

> She helped him memorize his first Scriptures, knelt with him daily as he recited his prayers, and explained the world to him in simple but distinctively Christian terms. He, in turn, adored her and regarded her every word as on par with the law of God. ... Years later, when he was under fire on some remote battlefield or entangled in the most troubling difficulties, he found himself praying the prayers he had learned at Mrs. Everest's knee.[22]

Churchill's belief that his country represented "Christian civilization" was central to his lifelong sense of mission, wrote Mansfield. "Growing inside him was his now historic, indomitable determination to stand and fight."

Some biographers assert that Churchill was an atheist, or agnostic, but Stephen Mansfield isn't one of them. He provides evidence in his biography that Churchill may have strayed from his Christian beliefs in his younger years, but not for long.

> Winston Churchill was a man of faith, a man who lived in the light of a vision unfashionably rooted in Scripture and centred in a sovereign God. He was a Christian, a man who passionately believed in the existence of truth, the reality of God, the power of His

Church, and the culture it produces.[23]

And so, when his day of destiny arrived, Winston Churchill was ready to lead the world with the faith, courage, tenacity, and moral excellence that he first learned from his beloved nanny, Elizabeth Everest. He described her as his dearest and most intimate friend in all his life.

Elizabeth Everest may remain unknown to the world at large. But heaven sings her praises. If it were not for her faithfulness to her calling– however insignificant it may have seemed in the eyes of others – Winston Churchill would never have become the leader and man that he did, and we would not be enjoying the resulting benefits of freedom and democracy.

You may have heard the famous line from an 1865 poem by Willaim Ross Wallace: "She who rocks the cradle rules the world." It is so true – there is nothing with more potential to influence society than the parenting, nurturing, and education of young children.

Elizabeth Everest never made headlines, yet her faithfulness left an indelible mark on history. In the same way, God has woven into your life a mission that is not measured by applause but by obedience. His purpose for you is redemptive, unique, and enduring—it cannot be revoked or erased.

But it must be cultivated through daily choices, even in the small and ordinary moments. When we nurture His purpose in our daily lives—whether through hidden service, quiet sacrifice, or bold obedience—we become part of His redemptive work in the world.

Living with divine purpose may not change the whole world, but it will change the part of the world God has entrusted to you. And as each believer embraces their calling, the ripple effect transforms generations. It's never too late to begin again, for God's mercies are new every morning. Will you step forward into your mission, trusting that the One who called you will also accomplish His work through you?

However, when He, the Spirit of truth, has come, He will guide you into all truth; for He will not speak on His own authority... and He will tell you things to come – Jesus.[24]

CHAPTER THREE
THE WELLSPRING OF VISION

If you have ever attended an in-person or online leadership conference or read one of the many thousands of books on leadership, you have no doubt heard or read this biblical quote: *"Where there is no vision, the people perish."*[25]

What do speakers and writers mean when they quote this verse of scripture?

In most cases, the emphasis is on human imagination, ideas, plans, and concepts. But those definitions have little to do with the meaning of the word *vision* when the first English Bibles were translated from Greek and Hebrew in the fifteenth and sixteenth centuries. At the time, *vision* literally meant *prophetic revelation, divine guidance,* or *divine dream*. The word's meaning has changed dramatically over the years, which is why many modern translations of the Bible, including the New King James version, use the word *revelation* instead of *vision.*

I like the ESV translation: *Where there is no prophetic vision the people cast off restraint, but blessed is he who keeps the law.*

There is a world of difference between human vision and divine revelation. As George Barna writes in his book, *The Power of Vision:*

> Vision developed by human beings suffers from tremendous limitations. The vision is limited by personal abilities and capabilities. It is filtered through societal and cultural boundaries and expectations. And it usually is limited in a serious way by the absence of spiritual perspective… God retains a call on everyone's life and ministry. While we have the ability to accept or reject that calling, He makes an understanding of the vision for our future available if we diligently seek it.[26]

Anyone can dream up a mental image of the future. But only a follower of Jesus Christ can receive divine revelation.

It's fine to have a mental vision of practical goals and desires like improving your health, becoming debt-free, or going on your dream vacation. But when it comes to purpose and destiny, the only vision that matters is the one that reflects God's purpose for you.

Where does your vision originate? If God is not your source, you might still achieve success in this world. But you will never become the man or woman God designed you to be. You will never fulfill His amazing call and purpose for your life if your vision is constrained within the boundaries of human wisdom. As God spoke through the prophet Isaiah:

> *"For My thoughts are not your thoughts, nor are your ways My ways," says the Lord. "For as the heavens are higher than the earth, so are My ways higher than your ways, and My thoughts than your thoughts."*[27]

Definitions of Vision

Common dictionary definitions include:

- a conception or image created by the imagination and having no objective reality
- something seen in a dream or trance
- a thought, concept, or object formed by the imagination
- the act or power of imagination
- unusual discernment or foresight
- an idea or mental image of something
- the ability to think about and plan for the future, using intelligence and imagination, especially in politics and business

There is nothing wrong with any of these definitions. After all, God gave us a brain, an imagination, and the ability to dream, plan, and strategize.

But God wants us to go beyond mere human imagination and tap into something with far greater potential to expand His kingdom: divine revelation.

Divine Revelation

How do we tap into God's higher thoughts and ways?

Several years ago, my husband and I went on one of my favourite hikes in the Rocky Mountains in western Canada. The trail started at the creek bed of the Sinclair

Canyon, where there is little to see other than the creek bed and the canyon walls. Because the sun is blocked by the canyon walls, the creek bed is dark, cool, and dreary.

After climbing higher, patches of sun glimmered through the surrounding forest. As we continued climbing up the trail, mountain tops became visible. Finally, we reached the top of the trail. To say the view was spectacular is a colossal understatement! We were surrounded by a vista of hundreds of mountains in the Sinclair and Rocky Mountain ranges that were hidden from view at the base of the canyon. I wish I could show you a picture – it was awe-inspiring and a perfect reflection of the majesty, beauty, and creativity of our Creator God.

The higher we climbed, the more we could see. Similarly, the more we get to know God, the broader and clearer our spiritual vision. The apostle Paul provides a beautiful illustration of this principle in his prayer for the Ephesian believers:

> *"...That the God of our Lord Jesus Christ, the Father of glory, may give you the spirit of wisdom and revelation in the knowledge of Him, the eyes of your understanding being enlightened; that you may know what is the hope of His calling, what are the riches of the glory of His inheritance in the saints."* [28]

According to <u>Strong's Exhaustive Concordance of the Bible</u>, the word *revelation* in this passage of scripture is translated from the Greek word *apokalupsis*, which means *laying bear, making naked,* and *disclosing truth about things before unknown.*

I like the *Message* paraphrase of this passage of

scripture, which says, "to make you intelligent and discerning in knowing him personally, your eyes and focused and clear, so you can see exactly what he is calling you to do."

God, who created you, knows you far better than you could ever know yourself. You can never truly know yourself—or your passions, gifts, and dreams—without also intimately knowing God. He *wants* to reveal His purpose for you.

Revelation of purpose unfolds over time, becoming more focused, clear, and detailed in stages as you continue in prayer, as you are faithful and obedient to everything God asks you to do, as you mature spiritually, and as you diligently seek God's guidance.

As we prioritize developing a closer relationship with Christ, the greater clarity we will develop of the rich treasures God has placed in us, and the vast horizons of purpose waiting for us to explore.

As you make this a priority, God will lift you to progressively higher vantage points of faith, where your spiritual vision is enlightened to your greater potential in Him.

How God Speaks

In the next chapter, we will look at the process by which vision develops, unfolds, and expands. For the remainder of this chapter, we will look at the most common ways that God speaks to us.

Scripture

The psalmist wrote, "Your word is a lamp to my feet and a light to my path."[29]

The Bible is God's instruction manual for life. He will lead, guide, and equip you through His word. That is the first place to look for direction. If you want to know how to become a better husband or wife, a better parent, more effective in your ministry or occupation, or better at hearing God – the Bible has lots to say about each of those areas.

Our attitude towards the scriptures also reflects our attitude towards God. Do I revere His word? Do I love His word? Am I hungry for His word?

When you open your Bible to read scripture, do so with an attitude of reverence and expectation. The scriptures are not just words on a page; they are powerful and transformative.

> *For the word of God is living and powerful, and sharper than any two-edged sword, piercing even to the division of soul and spirit, and of joints and marrow, and is a discerner of the thoughts and intents of the heart.*[30]

God's word is alive and full of divine power. This is the most common way that God speaks to His children. But we must be intentional about listening through reading, study, and meditation.

The Bible is also the standard for testing every other method by which God speaks. The Holy Spirit will never contradict His own word. He will never tell you it's okay to cheat on your income tax so you can give more money to missions. He'll never tell you it's okay to commit adultery or engage in other sexual sin. He'll never tell you it's okay to be bitter and resentful because of how badly someone hurt you.

If a thought or attitude or belief contradicts the

scriptures, it does not have its source in God.

Still small voice

You may be familiar with the Bible story of Elijah and how God told him to go out and stand on the mountain. The Bible says that God did not speak to Elijah in a dramatic way, through the wind, or an earthquake, or a fire. Rather, God spoke to Elijah in a "still small voice." Another translation says, in a "gentle and quiet whisper." [31]

God often speaks to me that way; not in an audible voice that I hear with my physical ears, but with a voice that I know and recognize in my spirit. This usually happens during prayer, Bible meditation, or worship. Sometimes it also happens when I go for walks in nature and focus on God's wonderful creation.

Jesus gave us a wonderful promise: "My sheep hear My voice, and I know them, and they follow Me."[32]

Notice Jesus does not say: My sheep *sometimes* hear My voice, or *some* of My sheep hear My voice, or *only the super-spiritual* hear My voice. If you belong to Christ, Jesus says you can hear His voice. It's not something weird or strange or only for the super spiritual prophets and evangelists. It's normal for every child of God.

If you are God's child, the question is not: does God speak? The question is, are you listening? Radio stations transmit signals twenty-four hours a day, seven days a week. But to hear them, we must turn on the receiver and tune in. Failure to hear the signal doesn't mean the station isn't transmitting.

And it's the same thing with hearing God. He is always

speaking.

As they ministered to the Lord and fasted, the Holy Spirit said, "Now separate to Me Barnabas and Saul for the work to which I have called them."[33]

Notice that the disciples were worshipping and praying and fasting when the Holy Spirit spoke. It is so important that we practise daily devotions to develop greater intimacy with God and deeper revelation of the scriptures, as this is key to learning how to discern and recognize the voice of the Holy Spirit.

Sometimes God's still small voice comes in the form of a picture or a vision in your spirit. For example, a Christian software engineer was praying for the solution to a programming problem. While she prayed, she saw a picture in her spirit, and it turned out to be just the solution she needed.

Someone asked a pastor, "What does God's voice sound like." I love his response: "God's voice sounds a lot like scripture, because God is the author of scripture."

Can you hear God's still small voice? Can you discern His gentle whispers? If you are intentional about getting to know God more, including reading, studying, and meditating on the scriptures, you will develop increasing sensitivity to the leading of the Holy Spirit.

Inner Witness

This is similar to a still small voice – but rather than words, it comes in the form of an inner witness. This witness occurs in your spirit, not your mind or emotions. As the Bible tells us:

The spirit of man is the lamp of the Lord.

> *The Spirit Himself bears witness with our spirit that we are children of God.*[34]

The inner witness is especially helpful when you need to make a decision but have not received clear direction from God. When that happens, it is helpful to first spend time in God's presence in prayer, the scriptures, and worship. Pray about the decision. Then, while in a spirit of prayer, imagine accepting the opportunity. What happens in your spirit? Do you experience an inner witness, a deep sense of peace, an assurance? Or is there an unsettledness in your spirit? This may manifest as a sense of heaviness or a check or warning.

The Holy Spirit will bear witness in our spirits, not our intellect. And the witness of the Spirit will always bring peace. As the apostle James wrote, "But the wisdom that is from above is first pure, then peaceable, gentle, willing to yield, full of mercy and good fruits." [35]

A word of warning here: some people think that experiencing God's peace means they will have no thoughts or feelings of fear. That is simply not true. Far from it. God wants us to live by faith, and He will often direct us to do things that are outside of our comfort zone. He may lead you to do something that terrifies you. God will confirm His direction with peace in your spirit, but you may still experience fearful thoughts and feelings.

I remember the very first time God directed me to accept an invitation to speak at a ladies' conference. It was the last thing in the world I wanted to do; public speaking terrified me. But as I prayed about it, God witnessed in my spirit that He wanted me to say *yes*. I still battled terrible fears and anxiety in the weeks leading up to the event.

But as I said *yes* to God then, and many times after that first event, God set me free from the fear of speaking. I still often feel nervous before speaking, but not fear. And I don't mind feeling nervous, because it keeps me dependent on God. At every point of my weakness, I embrace the grace and strength of Jesus.

It is vital that we do not let our emotions lead us; we must learn to develop such intimacy with God that we can differentiate between the leading of the Spirit and our emotions.

Seeking the inner witness has helped me on many occasions. I remember a time when I received two job offers. In the first offer, the company president named a salary way higher than the other, plus numerous benefits and other perks. The other offer included a generous salary, but it was not as high as the other.

I was tempted to accept the first offer. But as I spent time in prayer and sought the guidance of the Holy Spirit, I received a strong sense of *no* about the first offer, and a gentle, peaceful *yes* about the second. So I accepted the second offer, although I did question whether I made the right decision.

As it turned out, the company that made the first offer went bankrupt after one year.

The Holy Spirit knows things that we cannot possibly know in our minds. He knows the future. And no matter how good something looks, if God is not guiding you, it could lead to trouble and negative consequences.

Other people

When you are making a major life decision, it's wise to seek counsel from others *after* you have prayed and sought God on your own. Don't ask everyone for their opinion. But do talk to two or three people who are spiritually mature, know you well, and have proven qualities of wisdom and discernment. This is where humility comes in. We all have blind spots, and if you think you never make mistakes in hearing from God – well, that in itself is a major blind spot. As the writer of Proverbs tells us:

Where there is no counsel, the people fall;
But in the multitude of counselors there is safety.[36]

God may speak to you in a word of prophecy from someone. But the Bible warns that we must test the prophetic word. You have the Holy Spirit in you. If the prophecy is accurate, it will line up with the scriptures and it will resonate with your spirit.

Circumstances

There are times when God will cause certain circumstances to take place in our lives so that He can get a message to us. Sometimes this happens through encounters with people that God uses to develop our gifts and calling. Sometimes it's through an open door or closed door. That happened to Paul and his companions on one of their missionary journeys:

Now when they had gone through Phrygia and the region of Galatia, they were forbidden by the Holy Spirit to preach the word in Asia. After they had come to Mysia, they tried to go into Bithynia, but the Spirit did not permit them. So passing by Mysia, they came down to Troas. [37]

Some Christians base their decision-making

exclusively on the open-door policy. If a door of opportunity opens, they assume it must be God's will for them. Never assume that every open door is from God. Be sure and pray it through and make sure you have God's peace about stepping through that door.

Just as an open door is not in itself a sign of God's will, neither is a closed door always a sign that something is against God's will. God called one of history's greatest missionaries, William Carey, to take the gospel to India. But it was seven long years before he baptized his very first convert. Many of us would have given up after one or two years, assuming we misunderstood God's leading. But Carey never gave up.

Over the next twenty-eight years, Carey and his associates translated the entire Bible into India's major languages: Bengali, Oriya, Marathi, Hindi, Assamese, and Sanskrit and parts of 209 other languages and dialects. His greatest legacy was that he inspired the worldwide missionary movement of the nineteenth century.

God will use circumstances as one way of directing you – but He will also confirm it in other ways as well.

The more you train your spirit to discern and obey God's direction, the easier it will become to recognize His leading. Remember: God does not lead through emotions or your physical senses. Your emotions can lie to you. Your mind can lie to you. And the enemy will certainly lie to you. That is why the Bible tells us we must renew our minds by the word of God.

Commit yourself daily to developing your relationship with God, and you will become progressively more sensitive and discerning of God's voice and guidance.

Your word is a lamp to my feet
And a light to my path.[38]

CHAPTER FOUR
HOW VISION UNFOLDS

Don't you wish you could dial *1-800-Call-God* and get instant guidance for your future? Or ask God a question like you would ask for directions from the GPS in your car, and listen to a heavenly voice give you step-by-step instructions for where you need to go, what to do when you get there, and how to avoid pitfalls along the way?

When GPS first became available, I thought it was one of the best inventions ever. Why? Because I have never been able to read a map. It's one thing to look at the names of towns, cities, and tourist attractions. But interpreting the lines, routes, grids, and scales was like trying to read a foreign language.

Which made it all the more surprising to my family that I managed to navigate when I spent a year backpacking through Europe when I was twenty-one years old.

This might be hard for you to believe if you are under the age of thirty-five, but not only did I not have GPS – back then there were no tablets, cell phones, or internet. My navigation equipment consisted of an Eurail pass because I travelled by train, a selection of folded maps, and a directory of youth hostels. Also, I did not travel to English-speaking countries, because I wanted to experience new cultures. And since I didn't speak any language except English, that made it somewhat difficult to ask for directions.

Now you might be wondering: *If you couldn't read maps, and you couldn't speak the language, how did you get around?* Well, the way I got around was by using what I called the "point-and-smile" system. This is how it worked: when I arrived at a train station, I proceeded to the platform to find a friendly-looking passenger attendant. Then I would give him a big smile and point to the destination on the map. When he started to give directions, I would say the three words I had memorized in a few languages and say, "no speak French" (or German or Italian or Spanish, depending on my location).

At that point, the attendant would escort me to the correct platform and train to get to my destination. When I arrived at my destination, I would do the same thing – only this time pointing out the address of a youth hostel. And the attendant would direct me to the right train, subway, or bus. And guess what? My point-and-smile system worked perfectly.

When it comes to mission and purpose, most of us would love God to direct us like a heavenly GPS, with a clear picture of our destination, detailed instructions each step of the way, and warnings about obstacles to avoid. But it doesn't work like that. Purpose is a path, not a destination. And like any path, the view changes each step of the way.

"Your word is a lamp to my feet," wrote the psalmist, "and a light to my path."[39] At the time this psalm was composed, anyone venturing out at night would carry a lamp to avoid stumbling over obstacles, falling into an open sewer, or wandering off into paths that would lead to danger. The lamp guided each step, while the light (usually a torch) provided soft, general, illumination of the path ahead.

I am reminded of a late-night walk I took on a wooded mountain path near my parent's home in the Rocky Mountains. My flashlight lit the path directly before me, helping me avoid stumbling over a rock or snagging my foot in a gopher hole. A full moon glimmered through the partly overcast sky, casting muted illumination of the path ahead. After about a hundred feet, the path wound sharply to the right. Once I passed the corner, the moon lit up the next leg of the path, which veered up a sharp incline.

Like my flashlight, God guides my next steps, keeping me from stumbling or veering off in the wrong direction. And like the soft moon rays, He also provides general illumination of His broader purpose—enough direction to complete the present leg on my journey and to motivate and propel me forward to a future vision. Once I reach the next bend in the path, He will show me all the details I need to know to continue moving forward on my journey.

One thing God does not do, however, is illuminate all the details of my distant future.

When we study faith heroes in the Bible, we see that God rarely provided clear and detailed vision of their distant future. It's the same for you and me. Why? For one thing, we could not handle it. Some of us would run away in fear, and others of us would try and make it happen through our own strength and wisdom.

Most important, God wants to grow our faith. That means learning to trustfully depend on Him each step of the way. We need to develop the faith, integrity, courage, honesty, humility, wisdom, and spiritual maturity required to handle greater measures of influence and anointing.

Typically, God reveals purpose one step at a time, as we are faithful to steward the vision we have already received, and as our character and faith mature.

Do you become frustrated when you can't see very far ahead on your pathway of purpose?

Trusting God means obeying Him even when we don't understand what, where, when, how, or why. It means trusting Him with our future, confident that as we obey each step God sets before us, He will reveal additional vision and direction the moment we need to see it.

Purpose Unfolds Step-by-Step

Many Christians interpret words like *purpose, call, destiny, mission* as referring to a role, title, spiritual gift, or ministry position. But purpose is not a destination; it's a path. It is not one assignment; it's a series of assignments that lead to greater influence as we faithfully steward each one along the way. God reveals purpose incrementally as we walk in obedience, say yes to God, and steward each assignment He gives us.

Many people, not understanding this principle, give up on their dreams. They become frustrated when they can't see a detailed blueprint of their future. Others succumb to discouragement when they face obstacles and delays along the way.

God may give you broad vision of your calling. And He will always give you enough revelation to keep you walking in the right direction. But He will not show you each and every detail of the path ahead. He is looking for faith and trust, and your willingness to move forward step by step without knowing the entire destination.

Can you see why it is so important that when God directs you to take one step, you say *yes*? Otherwise, you will never see the amazing horizons of purpose waiting ahead. The problem is, some of us get to a particular point on the path, and we enjoy it so much that we decide to set up camp. We think: *Wow – I love this place. The view is spectacular, the people here are so nice, and they love me, and they tell me I'm doing a great job. I'm livin' the dream. I'm sure God must want me to stay here for the rest of my life.*

As a result, we are in danger of not discerning when God wants to lead us into new horizons of purpose waiting around the very next bend in the path. It is vital that we obey God each step of the way; as we do, He will reveal more vision the moment we need it.

Most biblical faith heroes discerned their calling progressively over time. Vision of their purpose, including specific details, unfolded and expanded over many years as they obeyed God each step along the way.

Remember Abram (who God later renamed Abraham)? When he first started on his faith journey, God gave him one instruction and one general promise. “Leave your homeland,” God said, “and go to the land I will show you.”[40]

Abram received no details about how to get to the land, where it was located, or what he was supposed to do when he arrived. All he received was one instruction and one promise that God would make Abram’s name great and bless all the nations of the earth through him. In other words, God gave him broad vision, and the next step that he was to take.

In a nutshell, God said, *Leave, go, and I’ll guide you and bless you.*

It was over many years, as Abram walked with God and obeyed each step along the way that he received greater clarity and details about his calling.

Was he perfect? Did he always obey and trust God? Far from it.

We often refer to Abram as a giant of faith. But he didn’t start out that way. He wasn’t born with any special gifts of faith. His family background wasn’t conducive to growing in faith. To the contrary, Abram’s family worshipped idols. He didn’t have anyone to teach him about God. He didn’t have a Bible or books or sermons or YouTube to teach him about faith.

Abram grew into a giant of faith over many years and even decades. He also made many mistakes during those years. At times he sinned and compromised. At other times he succumbed to fear, discouragement, and unbelief. And after becoming impatient when years had passed and there was no child, he tried to “help God out” and slept with Sarai’s maid, resulting in the birth of

Ishmael.

I'm glad the Bible records Abram's struggles. It gives me hope because I also battle times of discouragement, doubt, and unbelief. I also have sinned, compromised, and succumbed to fear on my faith journey. And if you're honest, so have you. But it was through his successes *and* his failures; it was through times of belief *and* times of doubt that Abram's faith and character matured and developed. God used all of Abram's choices and experiences to prepare his character to handle the blessings and responsibilities of the ultimate calling that God had for his life.

Make Friends with Discomfort

Is discomfort your friend or enemy? Most of us love our comforts. But to fulfill our call and destiny, we must learn to accept that discomfort will be part of the price we must pay.

Anyone with a dream to compete at the world Olympics knows there will be a price. They know that they will need to leave behind many comforts that most of us take for granted.

During the last Olympics, a journalist interviewed several athletes for a news story about what was involved in their training and preparation. He reported that they had worked out for an average of six hours a day, six days a week, fifty-one weeks a year. Those athletes accepted that discomfort would be part of the price for pursuing their life dream.

It was the same for Abram and Sarai. Not only did they have to leave behind the comforts of home, but their pathway of purpose involved one discomfort after another.

Before promising Abram that he would father a nation, God told him there was a pre-requisite: he had to leave his country and family and go.

What do you think that was like for Abram and Sarai? What did they have to leave behind?

Before I researched this topic, I never gave much thought to the sacrifices Abram and Sarai made to step into God's destiny. I knew they lived in a land of idolatry, but other than that, I imagined them living in a tent or cave or little grass hut.

I was wrong. Very wrong. Abram and Sarai lived in the city of Ur, in southern Mesopotamia, in what is now modern-day Iraq.

I discovered that Ur was no poverty-stricken little outpost in the middle of nowhere. It was a large and opulent city that drew its vast wealth from its position on the Persian Gulf, which gave it proximity to trade. The land was very fertile, and Mesopotamia was so rich in agricultural products that the crops provided way more than they needed to support the population. This allowed them to trade the surplus for other goods.

What were the homes like in Ur? Well, it turns out they were not tents or huts or caves. Archeological excavations have revealed that most homes in ancient Ur were large and comfortable. Consisting of baked mud brick, most were two or three stories high and some had more than a dozen or so rooms.

On the main floor of a typical home there was an open central courtyard with a fountain, surrounded by various domestic rooms. Those included a kitchen, usually equipped with a beehive shaped bread oven and cooking range, workrooms, a family room, a domestic chapel where cult structures and the family burial vault were kept, a reception area for guests, and a lavatory consisting of a stone floor with a hole in the middle. Some of the larger homes also had a full guest suite on the main floor with its own set of rooms and lavatory.

That gives you a better idea of what God was asking Abram and Sarai to leave behind. It couldn't have been easy for them.

I can't help but think it must have been especially hard for Sarai. If she is like most women, I'm sure she treasured her home. It was her place of refuge; it was there that she socialized with family and friends. I can imagine her thinking: *I'm supposed to leave all this? My beautiful home that I just re-decorated? My family? My relatives? Can we take any of the furniture? What about the family photo albums? Will there be any internet there – can I take my iPad and cellphone?*

Maybe she began to think, *I wonder...did old Abe REALLY hear from God? After all, he is seventy years old – maybe he's just getting a little senile and hearing voices. Why would God want us to start all over again, at our age? Where will we go? How will we get there?*

Remember – at this time God had provided no details about what the land would be like, what the journey would be like, or how they would get there. All Abram received was one instruction and one general promise.

Abram was seventy years old when he first received the call in Mesopotamia, but they moved to Haran for five years until his father died. He was seventy-five when they left Haran to travel to Canaan.

> *By faith Abraham obeyed when he was called to go out to the place which he would receive as an inheritance. And he went out, not knowing where he was going.*[41]

Is Father God prompting you to take a step of faith that requires pushing the boundaries of your comfort zone? Perhaps a step into something you can't see very clearly at this point? Does it feel scary, challenging, intimidating?

God is always wanting to lead us into more –more of His destiny, more of His purpose, and more of His power to minister to this hurting and broken world.

The comfort He asks you to leave behind may be external, like making a permanent move to the foreign mission field or ministering in a country where Christians are imprisoned and martyred for their faith, or leaving a prosperous career to serve in ministry, or running for political office and exposing yourself to unrelenting criticism.

For many of us, the comforts we need to leave behind are internal. Like the comfort of safety. The comfort of avoiding the risk of failure and feeling like a fool if things don't work out. The comfort of making sure we have all our ducks in a row before doing anything, convincing ourselves we're just being "responsible". The comfort of NOT confronting our fears. The comfort of having everyone speak well of us, thus avoiding the rejection and criticism that can come from sharing our faith or speaking politically incorrect truths about controversial issues. The comfort of silence, of being a nice, passive Christian who never rocks the boat.

Is there a comfort God is asking you to leave behind? How badly do you want to step into more of your potential and purpose? Do you want it badly enough to sacrifice comfort, safety, and security?

Faith plus Obedience = Miracles

We have had the privilege of a 35-year friendship as well the opportunity of doing ministry with a couple who are the best example I know of how faith and obedience cause vision to grow, expand, and multiply.

Their story is nothing short of miraculous, and shows how simply saying *yes* to God, then responding with faith, is an explosive combination that releases divine potential, power, and purpose. The story of their journey of faith and the amazing way that God has worked through their lives is told in their book, *Adventure, Romance & Revival.* [42]

Hazel Hill was born again at the age of 28, George at the age of 31. They joined a small church, but it split not long afterwards.

"Finally a few of us got together and decided we would be better off just meeting on our own, studying the Bible and praying for one another," Dr. George said. Revival filled their home, and many people were saved, healed, and delivered.

Before long, they outgrew their home and rented a community hall. Twenty-five people showed up for their first service on Mother's Day in 1979. Not long afterwards, they needed more space and rented first one ballroom in a hotel, then two, then three. Finally, they purchased an old Alliance church which seats about 350 people. The first service was so full they had to go to two services immediately.

By this time, it was obvious that a full-time pastor was needed. George had only been saved for three years, and he asked a PAOC pastor from Calgary to visit Lethbridge and consider pastoring the church. But after praying with them, he said he believed George and Hazel should take the leadership. The congregation unanimously asked them to pastor the church, and after prayer, they said *yes*.

"We really didn't have much idea of what we were doing, and we made some mistakes, but God blessed in spite of us," they recalled.

Both Dr. George and Dr. Hazel are powerful preachers, but it didn't start out that way. "One of the first times I tried to preach I stood up in front of sixteen people, looked at their faces, and my mind went blank," recalls Dr. George. "I had to ask Hazel to do it for me." But he kept facing this fear, and before long excelled as an anointed preacher.

To make a long story short, their church in Lethbridge grew to be one of the largest charismatic churches in Canada at that time. By 1988, five more churches were established in southern Alberta, and Victory Churches of Canada was formed.

We met Dr. George and Dr. Hazel about one year after they planted a church in northwest Calgary in January, 1990. At the opening service, 280 people showed up. The church grew quickly and within eighteen months there were four services on a Sunday, with about three to five hundred people in every service. Within a year, they planted three more churches in Calgary. With every church plant, they released about fifty people from the northwest church. “The Lord promised me years ago that for every leader I released, He would give me two of like quality and character and He has been faithful to do it,” Dr. George says. “Hazel and I have been blessed to have raised up many hundreds of ministers and great leaders.”

Victory Churches of Canada quickly became the largest church planting organization in North America. The organization's explosive growth rapidly expanded into the United States, Europe, Asia and Africa. They established numerous Victory Bible Colleges, Christian Schools, TV & radio ministries, orphanages, and women’s ministries including global outreaches to women and children.

At the time of writing, Victory Churches International had approximately two thousand churches in many nations around the world.

“Vision and dreams are the language of the Holy Spirit,” Dr. George said in an interview. “Obedience is our response to God’s guidance.”

Dr. Hazel added: “Step by step the way will open up before you. Every step of faith that we take brings us close to the fulfillment of the vision.” She referred to Proverbs 4:12: “When you walk, your steps will not be hindered, and when you run, you will not stumble.”

Are you ready to say yes?

What about you? Are you ready for more? Are you

willing to pay the price of leaving your comfort zone and pushing through criticism, obstacles, and fear to step into all that God has for you?

Each place on the pathway of purpose is important and it is vital that we are faithful with each assignment. But to experience the greater purpose God desires for us, when God says "move," we need to move. That means saying yes to God, time and time again.

God is full of surprises. And He has so much more for you than you can see right now. He wants you to dream, live the dream, and then dream again. Say *yes* to your Father, obey the next step, and you can be confident that He will lead you on an exciting path of greater horizons of purpose and adventure. God is faithful, and He will never let you down.

PART II: DISCOVER YOUR MISSION

PRACTICAL TOOLS TO HELP GUIDE YOUR DISCOVERY JOURNEY

I was worth about a million dollars when I was twenty-three and over ten million dollars when I was twenty-four, and over a hundred million dollars when I was twenty-five. And it wasn't that important because I never did it for the money. – Steve Jobs

CHAPTER FIVE
DISCOVERY TOOL: PASSION

If you follow the news, you will know that scientists are continually discovering new information about the universe.

In July 2022 for example, NASA released never-before-seen images of the universe obtained by the revolutionary James Webb Space Telescope (JWST). The following month, the telescope detected a galaxy that lies 35 billion light-years from Earth, which would make it the most distant galaxy ever found.

A more distant galaxy was captured by the telescope in 2024, which astronomers estimated to be more than 1,600 light years across, and the light is suspected to be coming from young stars. Astronomers also said the galaxy appears to be several hundreds of millions of times the mass of the sun.

In 2025, a team of astronomers using the telescope confirmed the most distant black hole ever observed, located inside a galaxy called CAPERS-LRD-z9. This black hole is estimated to be 50 million times the mass of the sun.

Every month or so, NASA continues to release new data and images.

"It sees things that I never dreamed were out there," senior project scientist and Nobel laureate John Mather said after the unveiling of the images.

Webb's telescope brought distant galaxies into sharp focus, revealing tiny, faint structures that had never been seen before, including star clusters and diffuse features.

Did these galaxies suddenly materialize out of nothing? No. They simply hadn't been seen before. As NASA Operations Project Scientist Jane Rigby said at a news briefing: "The universe, it's been out there. We just had to build a telescope to go see what was there."[43]

The more advanced the tools, the more scientists discovered. And as technology continues to evolve, scientists will discover even more galaxies in the future.

Purpose Tools

God has also provided tools for understanding our life purpose. Your gifts, calling, and purpose are already in you. You may lack clarity at this time, but thankfully, God has provided many tools to help you on the journey of discovery.

In the previous chapters, we looked at the characteristics of divine purpose and how it develops in our lives. My focus was on the spiritual aspects of how vision develops, including character development, spiritual maturity, prayer, faithfulness in stewarding each assignment God gives us, and the willingness to step out of our comfort zones.

In the next few chapters, we will look at several practical tools that will help you on the journey of discovering or re-discovering your mission. There are many practical tools and we can't cover them all; I will focus on those I consider most important.

Keep in mind that every part of the discovery process must be bathed in prayer. God, and God alone, is the source of divine vision and revelation.

The practical tools we will look at in the **Discover** section include passions, gifts, talents, personality, practical abilities, and life experiences.

Passion

The first discovery tool is passion. Passion is a powerful purpose-indicator, and the best place to start in the practical process of clarifying your purpose.

Did you know that God places passions in us to motivate us to pursue the calling He has for us?

> *For it is [not your strength, but it is] God who is effectively at work in you, both to will and to work [that is, strengthening, energizing, and creating in you the longing and the ability to fulfill your purpose] for His good pleasure.*[44]

Using your gifts in service to God should bring joy, not misery. Do you dread going to work each day? Is your ministry a heavy burden of drudgery? Is your favourite part of the day watching TV or Netflix, or chatting on social media? If so, you have not yet tapped into your passion.

Is there anything you do, or think about doing, that inspires you so much that you don't care about personal rewards or recognition?

Your economic situation or current responsibilities may not provide the option of matching your primary vocation to your passion, like Steve Jobs. But all of us can find some time to do those things God has uniquely wired us to do.

For the remainder of this chapter, you will explore your passions. As you work through the process, be careful to avoid allowing fear or self-doubt to hinder you from honestly and prayerfully searching your heart.

Invite God to probe the deepest places of your heart to unveil divine dreams and passions that are buried beneath the shrouds of inferiority, unbelief, self-doubt, and fear. Pray for revelation of what He wants to do through your life and ask Him to teach you to be a possibility thinker who dreams big and walks by faith.

If you truly desire to honour God, He will lead you. You can trust him with your most cherished hopes and dreams. Over time, you will gain greater clarity of God's purpose for your passions. Your calling will be a perfect fit for you. It will harmonize with your gifts, passions, personality, life experiences, and spiritual gifts.

As you work through this process, you may wonder,

How will I know if my passions are in alignment with God's purpose? The best answer to this question is found in Psalm 37:4: "Delight yourself in the Lord, and He shall give you the desires of your heart."

Christ must be your first and foremost passion. And getting the word of God in you is necessary for ensuring your heart passions line up with God's will and purpose. Jesus said:

> *If you abide in Me, and My words abide in you, you will ask what you desire, and it shall be done for you. By this My Father is glorified, that you bear much fruit; so you will be My disciples.*[45]

The more you get God's word in you, the more the desires of your heart will line up with God's desires, giving you the confidence to trust His promise: "I will instruct you and teach you in the way you should go; I will guide you with My eye."[46]

Create Dreamtime

The first step to identifying your passions is to set aside time to think, reflect, and pray. You may have already identified your passion(s) at some time in the past. But it is important to re-evaluate periodically and prayerfully, at least once a year. Whether your dream is clear or vague, whether your passion is strong, mediocre, or low – it is wise to periodically re-evaluate your passions and dreams.

This is your time to explore; for some of you it will be a re-exploration. As human beings we are constantly changing, and some people discover their primary passion may change over time, like my friend who loved singing more than anything for decades. But later in life, his greatest passion evolved to writing music and teaching young aspiring soloists.

That's why it is so important to set aside special time to wait in God's presence and invite Him to probe your heart and reveal the passions and gifts He has placed in you. Ideally, take a full day, or go away for a two or three-day personal retreat where you are free from distractions. During this time, take a mental and emotional step back from your current responsibilities. Remove thoughts of labels, titles, roles, positions, and job descriptions.

Imagine before you a blank canvas. Give yourself permission to draw something brand new on that canvas, something you have never drawn before. Give yourself permission to explore and dream of new possibilities.

Imagine that Jesus is inviting you to join Him on an adventure of dreaming and exploring. Dream without boundaries. Colour outside the lines. Free your imagination to dream new dreams with God.

Set aside parameters, rules, and boundaries. Silence the inner critic and fears. Refuse the temptation to come up with a list of obstacles of why something cannot be done or if it can be done, why you're not the person to do it. Write down everything that comes to mind, including anything that may seem silly, crazy, or ridiculous.

This is not the time to analyze if your passions are realistic, practical, or do-able. At this stage, you are *not* developing a plan of action. You are not writing a mission statement, a vision statement, or a list of goals. That will come later.

For those of you who think you know exactly what you are called to do, I encourage you to pretend you don't know. I want you approach this section as though you have no idea what your passions are. This will help you to be open to new ideas, thoughts, and creativity.

Simply write down everything that comes to mind.

Passion Discovery Questions

I have created questions to help you on this path of discovery. Take as much time as you need to answer as many questions as possible.

Here are a few guidelines for working through these questions:

-Don't worry about whether your answers to the questions are accurate. Some of these questions will require additional time in reflection and prayer to develop clarity.

-Avoid restricting your answers to occupational activities. Include personal activities and hobbies, as they will provide important clues.

-Be open to new ideas. You might think you already know your passions and dreams. At the very least, this approach will provide greater conviction and assurance of those passions.

-Refuse to compare yourself with others.

-Let go of other people's expectations. How many people attend law school because that's what their parents want? How many people become accountants because it is financially secure, when their deepest longing is to teach or nurse? How many people choose a profession because that is what everyone expects, when their heart's desire is to become a pastor?

"When I encounter teachers who are constantly complaining or meet housewives who are bitter, I quickly conclude that they are not following their divinely ordained mission," wrote Laurie Beth Jones in her book, *The Path*. "Perhaps they are following their economically ordained mission, or their culturally ordained mission, but they can't be following their divinely ordained mission, because bees hum while they work – they don't whine."[47]

Let's get started. We will look at three broad categories of passion: your joys, your sorrows, and the people groups you care about most.

Explore Your Joys

Get out your device or notebook and answer as many questions as you can:

- What makes you hum? What makes your heart sing? What excites and motivates you?
- What have you done, or thought about doing, that inspired creativity, ideas, and vision?
- What place or activity makes you feel most alive, passionate, and connected?
- Is there any activity that makes you so happy that you lose track of time?
- Is there anything you have done or are doing or that you think about doing that inspires you so much that you sometimes lie awake at night thinking about it – not because of worry or stress, but because of vision and excitement?
- What are your hobbies, and why do you like doing them?
- What do you enjoy doing in your spare time,

and why?

- What work, leisure, and volunteer/service activities have you found to be enjoyable and energizing?
- Which topics do you enjoy researching? What topics do you love to discuss with others?
- Read through a university course catalogue. If you had the time, which courses would you love to study? If you had the opportunity to start your education all over again, what would you study?
- Is there anything you have a desire to influence and change, such as the education system, poverty, human trafficking?
- What do you find yourself daydreaming about?
- Is there anything that you do, or think about doing, or pray about doing, that creates a deep inner assurance: *this is what I was born to do?*
- If there were absolutely no constraints, such as time, money, skills, and resources, and you knew you could not fail, what would you do?
- Ask people who know you well, "When do I seem the happiest? What do I do most enthusiastically?"
- Does time seem to fly by when you engage in a certain activity? What is it?
- Is there something you would love to do even if you were not paid for it?

"Painters must want to paint above all else," said researcher Mihaly Csikszentmihalyi, a University of Chicago psychologist. Professor Csikszentmihalyi conducted a study of two hundred artists, first in art school, and then eighteen years later. He found that the artists who savored the sheer joy of painting became serious painters. But those who were drawn to the profession in hopes of wealth or fame eventually drifted to other professions.

"If the artist in front of the canvas begins to wonder how much he will sell it for, or what the critics will think of it, he won't be able to pursue original avenues. Creative achievements depend on single-minded immersion."[48]

Explore Your Sorrows

What does sorrow have to do with passion? More than you might think. Most people equate passion with feelings of happiness and excitement. But passion is defined as any powerful or compelling emotion. And that includes sorrow, anger, and compassion.

Achieving something of significance generally involves doing something that represents the solution to a problem, or a way of meeting a need you care deeply about, and more importantly, that God cares deeply about.

Often, connecting with a problem and allowing yourself to feel the pain and suffering of other people will be the very thing that leads you to your dream.

Candace Lightner's dream was conceived in sorrow, after her thirteen-year-old daughter, Cari, was killed by a drunk hit-and-run driver in 1980. It was not the driver's first drunk driving accident; he had been arrested a short time earlier for another incident related to drunk driving. After police officers told Lightner that the driver would not likely receive much punishment for killing Cari, she became enraged. She decided to channel her anger and grief into fighting drunk driving, and she formed MADD –

Mothers Against Drunk Driving.

Since 1980 MADD has raised awareness of drunk driving and successfully lobbied for tougher laws against offenders.

Martin Luther King Jr. is perhaps the most famous historical example of someone whose dream emerged from intense sorrow. He was heartbroken over the widespread oppression of his fellow black Americans who were forced to sit at the back of the bus, not allowed to eat at restaurants frequented by white clientele and not permitted to use public drinking fountains. He was angry that young black children were forced to attend segregated schools that provided a substandard level of education.

Martin Luther King Jr. identified with the pain and heartache of suffering humanity. He opened his heart to God's heart, feeling the deep compassion and grief that our heavenly Father feels when any man, woman, or child suffers injustice, abuse, and oppression.

Out of Rev. King's broken heart was birthed a vision of His destiny. He dreamt of a nation where all people would truly be equal, where little boys and girls would be judged not by the colour of their skin, but by the content of their character.

"I have a dream," he said in his famous speech at the Lincoln memorial in 1963 in Washington, D.C. "I have a dream that one day this nation will rise up and live out the true meaning of its creed: 'We hold these truths to be self-evident, that all men are created equal'."

Martin Luther King knew his dream might cost him his life. And it did, when five years later he was assassinated.

But his dream also inspired a revolution in civil rights that literally transformed a nation. Although there is still much more that needs to be done to achieve true racial equality, to this day, those four words from his famous speech still reverberate through every generation around the world: "I have a dream."

Many people never tap into their dream because they turn a blind eye to the pain of suffering humanity. None of us enjoy feelings of pain, and it's all too easy to harden our hearts and ignore the injustice in our world.

Pray for God's heart for others. Then ask yourself the following questions:

- Is there anything that stirs in you a deep holy anger or intense grief and compassion for other people, for example, injustice, poverty, AIDS, child abuse?
- Is there anything about the world or human suffering that spurs you to want to do something? It might be something of a global nature, like human trafficking, the plight of children manipulated into the sex trade, or children in developing countries who lack education, food, and housing. It may be something local, like kids in single parent families, the challenges of new immigrants, or the plight of the poor and homeless. It might be physical or mental illness, grief, anxiety, poverty, loneliness, or anxiety. It might be the emotional and spiritual suffering that people experience who have never found the freedom and wholeness that can only come through a relationship with Jesus Christ.

- Is there anything you have a passion to influence and change, such as in the education system, media, business, politics?
- Is there anything about human suffering that literally breaks your heart? Don't run from it. Don't ignore it or try and disconnect from the pain. Embrace the grief of humanity, and pray, *"Father, is there is something that you want me to do in this situation?"*
- Have you had a deeply painful experience that has given you the desire to help others who are suffering from something similar? (We will explore the role of life experiences in chapter seven).

Identify People Groups

Another key that will help clarify your passions is to think about people you would like to help. Most Christians feel compassion for anyone who suffers. But is there one category of suffering people that crushes your heart? Here are some examples of people groups (this is not an exhaustive list).

- Homeless people
- People with disabilities
- The poor
- Children forced into sexual slavery
- Children in single-parent families
- People grieving over the loss of a loved one
- People in spiritual bondage
- New immigrants
- People groups in your church, such as youth, children, or the elderly
- People suffering injustice

- Corrupt governments
- Unwed mothers
- Orphans
- Troubled teens
- People with a mental or physical illness

Avoid the temptation to protect yourself from the pain of others. Embrace it. Immerse yourself in it. Learn about it. For example, if people suffering from AIDS really breaks your heart, research online to learn more about it. Then volunteer at an AIDS hospice and talk to people suffering from AIDS. Talk to their caregivers. You could very well find your destiny.

Look into the face of pain, embrace the grief of humanity, and pray, *Father is there something you want me to do to use my passion and gifts to meet a need that you care deeply about?*

Passion to Persevere

"Passion is a critical element for anyone who wants to achieve a dream," said John Maxwell, international author of numerous best-selling books on leadership. "It is the starting point of all achievement. I've never seen anyone achieve anything of any value – without the spark of passionate desire. It provides the energy that makes dreams possible."

Does your passion *compel* you to follow it? Merriam-Webster defines *compel:* to drive or urge forcefully or irresistibly. It's a verb that is almost always associated with action.

"If you are working on something you really care about, you don't have to be pushed," said Steve Jobs. "The vision pulls you."

Anyone who follows a big dream will encounter many obstacles, setbacks, and disappointments along the way. It will take time, effort, and a whole lot of perseverance. If your dream does not compel you to follow it, you're more likely to give up when you face inevitable delays and disappointments along the way.

Passion is the fuel that will help you persevere.

Remember, God sees unlimited potential in you. He sees impossible dreams coming to pass through His power and grace working through you. When He looks at you, he envisions the woman or man you can become through his transforming power.

I love the way author Greg Levoy describes passion: "Passion is what we are most deeply curious about, most hungry for. It is whatever we pursue merely for its own sake, what we study when there are no tests to take, what we create though no one may ever see it."

So once again – do you have a passion that compels you to follow it? Is your passion still burning strong? And if not, why not? Have you lost clarity and focus? Have distractions, difficulties, stress, criticism, or delays quenched your passion? If so, how can you rekindle it?

By far the most important way you can tap into your passions is to draw closer to Jesus. After all, God made you; he is the one who planted desires and gifts in your heart. Regardless of how deeply those desires are buried or how often they have been trampled on through the years, the resurrection power of Jesus Christ can release them to grow and blossom.

Ask God to illuminate the passions he placed in your heart. Ask him to unearth divine dreams that may be buried under the rubble of disappointment and failure. Trust His grace to heal broken areas of your heart that may be suppressing your deepest desires.

God is faithful, and He will help lead you in the journey of discovering your truest heart passions.

Your spiritual gifts were not given for your own benefit but for the benefit of others, just as other people were given gifts for your benefit – Rick Warren.

CHAPTER SIX
DISCOVERY TOOL #2: GIFTS & TALENTS

It has been said that the truest evidence of a gift is having a passion for it. And while that is mostly true, there are plenty of exceptions. If you have ever watched *Britain's Got Talent or American Idol*, then you'll know what I mean.

Why else would so many people with absolutely no singing talent stand in long lines and appear on national television when they clearly have no chance of winning? Why would they subject themselves to public mockery, criticism from the judges, and the boos and laughter of the audience?

I have no doubt the show producers accept many applicants with no singing talent because train-wreck auditions are entertaining. But I can't help but wonder: *Don't those contestants have a friend or family member who loves them enough to tell them the truth?* After all, they must pay their own expenses, as the only contestants who receive compensation are those who make it to the top ten.

On the other hand, there are men and women that nobody has ever heard of – people who never saw themselves as doing anything special or spectacular or winning international recognition– who became overnight sensations.

One such person is Susan Boyle. A 47-year-old charity worker who lived a simple life in a small village in Scotland, she loved to sing but had never sung before a larger audience than her small Catholic parish. After she won several small local singing competitions, her mother urged her to enter *Britain's Got Talent* and take the risk of singing in front of an audience larger than her parish church. She was reluctant as she felt she was too old; she believed one had to be young, attractive, and fashionable to win. But her former coach finally convinced her to apply for an audition.

I still remember that episode, when Susan walked awkwardly on stage, looking frumpy and overweight in a dowdy dress, with unkempt hair and no makeup. Host Simon Cowell, in his famously condescending style, asked Susan some pre-performance questions. She told the show's cameras that she lived alone with her cat, *Pebbles*, and had "never been kissed."

The show's cameras caught many people in the predominantly young audience rolling their eyes and snickering at Boyle's words and appearance. Everyone, including the judges, expected her to make a fool of herself.

Then she opened her mouth and began to sing. What happened next was a powerful lesson in not judging a book by its cover. As Susan belted out, *I Dreamed a Dream* from Les Misérables, the judges looked startled; the audience looked shocked, then rose in a standing ovation.

Judge Piers Morgan said afterwards, "When you stood there with that cheeky grin and said, 'I want to be like Elaine Paige' everyone was laughing. No one is laughing now."

Boyle became an overnight sensation, and within two days, the YouTube video of her performance had more than 35 million views. Piers Morgan later said, "She had the voice of an angel."

"We prejudged her by her looks and we were fooled," wrote author Peter Bregman in a guest column for CNN. "But there was something Susan Boyle awakened in us, as we watched her come out of her shell. Who among us does not move through life with the hidden sense, maybe even quiet desperation, that we are destined for more? That underneath our ordinary exterior lies an extraordinary soul? That given the right opportunity, the right stage, the right audience, we would shine as the stars we truly are?"[49]

What about you? Do you have gifts you have not developed or shared with the world because you think you are too old, too young, not attractive enough, or not talented enough? Do you look at others more talented than you and hide your gift, because you feel inadequate in comparison?

Or, instead of developing your own gifts and talents, do you try and mimic others you admire? I can't help but wonder how many of us are living someone else's dream in an attempt to win love and acceptance from others. Some people invest so much time and energy trying to be like someone else, they never take the time to discover and develop their own unique gifts and talents.

Don't be an echo; be a voice. You are special and one of a kind. A vital element in discovering your purpose is to be true to yourself and honour your raw material. God will not empower you to live someone else's dream. He will only empower you to be who He created you to be and do what He has called you to do.

"As a crucial part of your calling, you were given certain gifts, talents, longings, and desires," wrote John Ortberg in *If You Want to Walk on Water You've Got to Get Out of the Boat*. "To identify these with clarity, to develop them with skill, and to use them joyfully and humbly to serve God and his creation is central to why you were created."[50]

Gifts: Spiritual or Natural

Over the years, many theologians have debated about the differences between natural gifts and spiritual gifts. Some say that the natural gifts you are born with are completely different from spiritual gifts, and that only the gifts we receive after becoming a Christian can be considered 'spiritual'.

We have all heard stories or watched examples on Facebook or YouTube of young children demonstrating phenomenal musical ability. I know of a gentleman who started playing complex pieces on the piano as a five-year-old, with no sheet music and no training. That child later grew up to become a powerful, anointed worship leader.

Some would say that the child was born with that talent, and it is therefore a natural ability and not a spiritual gift. But is it not also a spiritual gift since he later used it to lead people to Christ and build God's kingdom?

Some gifts we are born with; these are called motivational gifts and are described in Romans chapter twelve. Motivational gifts reside in you; they are God-given traits and abilities that provide the inherent driving force behind our choices and actions. Although you were born with these gifts, they do not become released into their God-intended purpose and potential until you come to faith in Christ.

Let's take a closer look at the different types of gifts. If you have never taken a spiritual/motivational gifts test, I encourage you to do so. Spiritual gifts can be divided into three broad categories: *Equipping gifts, manifestation gifts, and motivational gifts.*

1 - Equipping Gifts

The equipping gifts include apostle, prophet, evangelist, pastor, and teacher. These are people God has called to ministry leadership within the global and local church. Their job is to equip believers for the work of ministry, and to build maturity in the congregation. Paul explains the purpose of the leadership gifts:

> *And He Himself gave some to be apostles, some prophets, some evangelists, and some pastors and teachers, for the equipping of the saints for the work of ministry, for the edifying of the body of Christ, till we all come to the unity of the faith and of the knowledge of the Son of God,*

to a perfect man, to the measure of the stature of the fullness of Christ..."[51]

2 – Manifestation Gifts

The manifestation gifts represent the work of the Holy Spirit through the life of a believer in a given situation to demonstrate God's love and supernatural power. All Spirit-filled believers can operate in the manifestation gifts. These gifts are listed in 1 Cor. 12:4-6 and include prophecy, tongues, interpretation, wisdom, knowledge, discernment, faith, healings, and miracles. Unlike motivational gifts, these gifts are not resident in a believer; they reside in the Holy Spirit and operate as the Spirit wills.

"But one and the same Spirit works all these things, distributing to each one individually as He wills."[52]

3 – Motivational Gifts

Charles Stanley explains the purpose of the motivational gifts this way: "A motivational gift is the driving force that causes you to do the things you do the way you do them."

The motivational gifts are especially significant for discovering and clarifying your purpose. The seven motivational gifts are described in Romans chapter 12 and include: perceiving (prophecy), serving, teaching, encouraging, giving, leading, and mercy.

For as we have many members in one body, but all the members do not have the same function, so we, being many, are one body in Christ, and individually members of one another. Having then gifts

> *differing according to the grace that is given to us, let us use them: if prophecy, let us prophesy in proportion to our faith; or ministry, let us use it in our ministering; he who teaches, in teaching; he who exhorts, in exhortation; he who gives, with liberality; he who leads, with diligence; he who shows mercy, with cheerfulness.* [53]

Your motivational gift will match your passion, and every Christian has at least one. As already mentioned, your motivational gift was resident in you at birth, but you must have a relationship with Christ for it to be released into God's purpose.

They are called motivational gifts because that is what they do: they motivate you. They inspire you. They galvanize you in your service to God.

I strongly urge you to complete a motivational gifts assessment. These usually identify not just one, but your top three gifts. While you will have one gift that will be your prominent motivation and function, your second and third gifts will complement your primary gift.

Simply google "motivational gifts test" and you'll find lots of resources. Or check with your pastor or local church to see if they have a test you can take.

The Bible says that everyone has received a gift. Everyone! Now, your gift may not seem like much compared to other people. But if you thank God for it, develop it, and share it with others, God will multiply its effectiveness!

As Paul told Timothy, "Therefore I remind you to stir up the gift of God which is in you... For God has not given us a spirit of fear, but of power and of love and of a sound mind."[54].

What is the purpose of your gift? To serve others and build God's kingdom:

> *As each has received a gift, use it to serve one another, as good stewards of God's varied grace: whoever speaks, as one who speaks oracles of God; whoever serves, as one who serves by the strength that God supplies—in order that in everything God may be glorified through Jesus Christ. To him belong glory and dominion forever and ever.* [55]

Get to know how God uniquely wired and gifted you. What you are is God's gift to you. What you do with yourself is your gift to God and to the world.

Many people tend to think of spiritual gifts as restricted to public gifts like worship, teaching, preaching, and pastoring. But these only scratch the surface of the gifts in the body of Christ.

One example is the motivational gift of mercy, often reflected in an ability to listen and show empathy. While all of us need to be compassionate and become better listeners, some people have a unique ability to make everyone they communicate with feel affirmed, valued, and encouraged. By listening with empathy and compassion, they draw the best out of others. As the writer of Proverbs wrote, "The purposes of a person's heart are deep waters, but one who has insight draws them out."[56]

Your gift may be of a more practical nature. Perhaps you have a technical gift and enjoy managing multi-media at your church. Or, you might have a gift for administration, and you enjoy planning, organizing, and managing details.

Motivational gifts can also be used in a secular

setting. For example, a Christian doctor may have the motivational gift of encouraging, a special ability to call forth the best in others through motivation, exhortation, and encouragement. If that doctor seeks to use that gift in their medical practice to glorify Christ, God will work through him or her to minister to their patients. It may result in someone experiencing salvation, or seeking out a church community, or it may simply soften their heart to be more receptive to the Holy Spirit drawing them. We must be careful not to limit God; instead let's view every situation as an opportunity to use the gifts He has given us to serve others.

I know of a Christian businessman with a shepherding gift, and he uses that gift to provide pastoral care and counseling to his employees (I tell the story about this gentleman in chapter 9). My sister, who is a mature woman of God and full of the Holy Spirit, has a motivational gift of serving, reflected primarily in hospitality. She loves to cook meals not only for family and friends, but also for those who are poor, sick, bereaved, or discouraged. And through that gift, she has had opportunities to minister in other ways with encouraging words and sharing Christ.

The gifts of preaching, teaching, pastoring, or leading worship are of no more value to God than the gifts of administration, listening, encouraging, compassion, serving, or intercession.

What matters is that we steward and develop what God has given us. As Paul wrote in the letter to the Colossians: "And whatever you do in word or deed, do all in the name of the Lord Jesus, giving thanks to God the Father through Him."[57]

Skills

Skills are different from spiritual gifts. They might reflect a person's talent or gift, but not always. For example, I am skilled at administration, because I needed to develop that skill when I ran my own business. But it is not a gift. How do I know? I hate it. An hour spent on administrative tasks leaves me feeling more tired and drained than eight hours doing something I am passionate about. On the other hand, I have a bookkeeper friend who says that when she is feeling stressed or tired, logging on to her accounting software and spending a couple of hours bookkeeping never fails to energize and refresh her.

How do you know whether your skill is a gift? Ask this question: *Does it motivate me? Does it energize me? Or does it leave me feeling drained and empty?*

Personality Type

God gave you a unique personality that, together with your spiritual gifts, natural talents, passions, and life experiences plays a part in the purpose He designed for you.

There are lots of resources on the internet for doing personality tests. One of the highest rated is Myers Briggs —you can do an online test for a fee. Another popular fee-based test is DISC (go to Discprofile.com).

There are also some free assessments; many people have found a free assessment by Enneagram to be quite accurate (go to Enneagramcoach.com).

Evaluate

-Describe the results of your spiritual gifts test.

-What are your three top motivational gifts?

-Which skills, gifts, and interests match your passions? Which do not?

-What is your personality style based on the assessment you completed?

-Describe your top two or three skills, gifts, or interests that match your passions.

You have been entrusted with a one-of-a-kind blend of talents, gifts, skills, and personality. They were never meant to lie dormant or remain hidden. They are God's investment in you, intended to bless others and to advance His Kingdom. Do not rob the world by taking those talents to the grave with you. When you discover and steward them faithfully, you step into the joy of living aligned with your divine design.

The question is not *if* your life will make a difference, but *what kind* of difference it will make. Begin today to lean into your unique gifts and trust God to multiply their impact far beyond what you imagine.

And we know that all things work together for good to those who love God, to those who are the called according to His purpose.[58]

CHAPTER SEVEN

DISCOVERY TOOL #3: LIFE EXPERIENCE

Several years ago, I watched a YouTube video showing a young man skateboarding, golfing, swimming, playing an instrument, and holding his baby son. You may be wondering, *Why would you waste your time watching a guy doing such ordinary, everyday activities?*

I watched the video for the same reason several million other people watched it – this young man had no arms, and no legs. So, when I saw him zipping around on his skateboard with no legs and playing an instrument or using a driver to hit a golf ball with no arms, I took notice.

Nick Vujicic is doing things that some of the world's top medical specialists said he could never do. But it wasn't always that way.

As a child, Nick was mocked and bullied at school for

having no arms or legs. That led to depression, and when he was only ten years old, he wanted to commit suicide. As Nick shared his story at New Hope Church in Oahu, he said, "I asked God, 'God, if you love everyone and you love me, why did you give me less? Why didn't you give me arms and legs? And since we know that the God we serve is a God of miracles, I prayed for a miracle."[59]

For several years, Nick wondered, *Why God, was I born this way? I don't understand how you can say that You love me when You allow me to stay in this pain.*

He received his answer at age fifteen when God spoke to him through the story of the blind man in John chapter nine. When the disciples asked Jesus why the man was born blind, assuming it was due to either the man's sin, or the sin of his parents, Jesus responded, "Neither this man nor his parents sinned, but that the works of God should be revealed in him."

Nick says, "I'm like, wow God, if you had a plan for the blind man, you do have a plan for me. That was the beginning of my relationship with Jesus." [60] He realized that if God made him that way, his disabilities could never stand in the way of him living a full and purposeful life.

And oh my, did God ever have a purpose! His disabilities and painful life experiences became the very things that launched a world-wide platform for sharing the gospel of Jesus Christ. And since his first speaking engagement at the age of nineteen, Nick has traveled all around the world, sharing his story with tens of millions of people. Already, this young evangelist has accomplished more than most people achieve in a lifetime.

I love Nick's story, because it shows what God can do when we give Him our brokenness and painful experiences and trust Him to work them together for good.

Do you sometimes feel you are too broken, weak, or flawed for God to work through you to minister to others? Do you constantly belittle yourself about your weaknesses or perceived lack of talent? Do you wish God made you differently? Do you wish you had a different personality, a different body, a different face, a different family background? Do you feel ripped off by circumstances in your life?

When I wrote my first book, I fell into the trap of comparing myself to others. While I had achieved a fair amount of success as a magazine journalist, this was different. Now I would be writing a book to encourage and teach others to become whole in Christ. But who was I to think I could do that? I felt intimidated by all the amazing Christian authors whose books I had read. I felt so inadequate.

It was during prayer that God spoke to my heart and reminded me of Jesus' words to Paul when he repeatedly prayed that God would remove the thorn in his flesh: "My grace is sufficient for you, for My strength is made perfect in weakness."

How did Paul respond? He said, "Therefore most gladly I will rather boast in my infirmities, that the power of Christ may rest upon me."[61]

I realized that it was not about me; it was about Christ in me and His Spirit working through me to minister to others and accomplish His purpose. My job was to do what God directed me to do and trust Him with the outcome.

Some of the most powerful demonstrations of God's power and purpose occur through people who are the most broken and weak; those who have suffered the worst tragedies, the greatest opposition, or the most persecution. Although none of us like to feel weak, that is the very place where we can most fully experience God's strength.

God often chooses the unlikely. He chose a prostitute, a tax collector, a murderer of Christians. He chose Moses, a reluctant leader. He chose Gideon, a terrified warrior hiding in a winepress. When God called him, Gideon said: "O my Lord, how can I save Israel? Indeed my clan is the weakest in Manasseh, and I am the least in my father's house."

How did God respond? "Surely I will be with you, and you shall defeat the Midianites as one man."[62]

God chose Abraham, who eventually matured in his faith so much that the New Testament describes him as the "father of faith." But twice, he was so weak in his faith that he told his wife to lie to protect himself. He also became impatient waiting for the promised son and slept with his wife's maid to try and force the fulfillment of God's promise with his own plan.

God chose a king who committed adultery with Bathsheba and murdered her husband to cover up his sin. Yet God described David as "a man after my own heart." He is the only person in the Bible to earn that description. Amazingly, although the first child born to David and Bathsheba died as punishment for David's sin, their second son was Solomon, through whom came the lineage of Christ.

In chapter two (*What is Divine Mission?*), I described several characteristics of purpose; one of those is that purpose is redemptive. Redemptive purpose is the miracle by which God takes every life experience and area of brokenness that we surrender to Him and works it all together for good.

> *And we know that all things work together for good to those who love God, to those who are the called according to His purpose.*[63]

The worst thing that has happened to you, the very thing that others intended to harm you, or Satan meant for evil, God can turn around and use to launch you into a powerful destiny. You can trust Him to bring good out of every tragedy, heartache, betrayal, and shattered dream.

That is why your life experience is a vital purpose-indicator. God loves to pour His power into our areas of weakness. He loves to transform disappointments into destiny. He loves to show Himself strong on our behalf.

What life experiences have had the greatest impact on you? Both positive and negative experiences can help point you to your purpose, especially negative experiences. The remainder of this chapter will focus on life experience discovery questions.

Your Positive Experiences

- What are your favourite memories from childhood?
- Was there a school or college project that introduced you to an exciting new interest,

regardless of the grade you received? Describe.

- Have you had any positive experiences that might connect to your passion or gift?
- Recall a time you did something you were proud of. What did you do, and why did it make you feel proud?
- Have you engaged in any volunteer activities that gave you a strong sense of purpose? Describe.
- If you enjoy your occupation or ministry, describe what aspects bring you the greatest joy.
- Look back over the last five years of your life. What positive activities or events made you feel strong, engaged, and purposeful?

Your Painful Experiences

- Reflect on your childhood. What experiences caused you the greatest pain?
- Describe painful experiences from your teenage and young adult years and how they affected you.
- Have you had a deeply painful experience that has given you the desire to help others who are suffering through something similar?
- Have you experienced a traumatic loss, such as the sudden death of a close family member? How did it affect you?
- What other difficult hardships have you faced, such as abuse, failure, betrayal, divorce, serious illness in yourself or another family member?
- Describe other adversities or obstacles you have endured. What strengths helped you to

overcome them?
- Which painful experiences gave you greater empathy to help others suffering through the same adversity?
- Describe positive changes in your character, attitude, or spiritual life that occurred as a result of persevering through adversity.
- How can those positive changes help others who experience similar adversities?

Adversity is often intertwined with calling. Why? Suffering motivates us to depend on Jesus for healing and restoration. This helps prepare us to help others who are suffering through similar circumstances.

> *Blessed be the God and Father of our Lord Jesus Christ, the Father of mercies and God of all comfort, who comforts us in all our tribulation, that we may be able to comfort those who are in any trouble, with the comfort with which we ourselves are comforted by God. For as the sufferings of Christ abound in us, so our consolation also abounds through Christ.*[64]

It has been said: *Adversity can make you bitter or better*. You have no doubt experienced one or more major adversities in your life. Those experiences, once processed, will give you greater empathy and compassion to help others who undergo similar experiences.

Adversity can build us or crush us. It can strengthen our faith or weaken it. It can help or hinder us in fulfilling God's divine purpose in our lives.

I'm reminded of a man I met a few years ago after I spoke at a church in Kauai. He stood out in the crowd because he looked like a jolly old Santa Clause. His eyes twinkled; he wore a big smile and seemed to bubble over with effervescent joy. I guessed his age to be in the mid-to-late seventies.

As we chatted, he told me that he and his wife moved to Kauai from the mainland just a few months prior. I asked, “Are you retired?” He said, “Well, sort of. That was the plan. But you know, we just love kids too much to retire.” Then he told me a touching story that reminded me of how God can use our disappointments for a higher purpose.

He and his wife loved children and planned to have a big family. But the years went by, and they were unable to have children of their own. They prayed and prayed for healing; they saw medical doctors, but nothing changed.

Finally, they decided to take in a foster child. Then another. Then a few more. They built a big house with lots of bedrooms, including a swimming pool with a huge yard to play in. Over the years, they adopted several children and fostered over a hundred more. “If we could afford it, we would have adopted the whole bunch,” he said.

They loved the children as though they were their own. They trained them in practical life skills, taught them about God’s love, and showed them how to treat each other. All the kids called them papa and mama, even when they became adults.

He shared stories of kids from many different backgrounds, including some desperately sad situations, and the joy of loving these kids and planting the seeds of faith.

Through all these experiences, they realized that

loving and raising orphans and hurting children was their life calling. Although it was a lot of work, they loved every minute of it.

In time, this couple moved to Kauai to retire. But that didn't last long. They missed children so much that they became involved in a business that cares for kids whose parents are vacationing in Kauai and need childcare. Children from all over the world are coming to their home and experiencing the love of God in action.

God didn't give this couple what they had originally asked for – their own babies – because He had a greater purpose in store. And it's the same for us. Sometimes we can become bitter or resentful over seemingly unanswered prayers. But if you are willing to surrender your disappointments to Him, there will come a time when you say: *Thank you Father – this is so much better than my plan.*

In chapters two and four, I shared some other stories about how God can use our painful experiences for a beautiful purpose.

Your painful life experiences are an important key to unlocking your life purpose. No matter what happens to us, God is able to work it together for good. His plans for us are always good, even if the path to that purpose involves pain and sorrow.

As God said through the prophet Isaiah:

For My thoughts are not your thoughts,
Nor are your ways My ways," says the Lord.
"For as the heavens are higher than the earth,
So are My ways higher than your ways,
And My thoughts than your thoughts.

For as the rain comes down, and the snow from heaven,
And do not return there,
But water the earth,
And make it bring forth and bud,
That it may give seed to the sower
And bread to the eater,
So shall My word be that goes forth from My mouth;
It shall not return to Me void,
But it shall accomplish what I please,
And it shall prosper in the thing for which I sent it.[65]

His ways, His thoughts, are so much higher than mine, or yours. But he is faithful. He promises that His word will not return void. He promises that if you trust Him, He will accomplish a wonderful purpose in and through your life.

God always keeps His promises – in His way, and in His time.

There is nothing in your life– not your past, mistakes, failures, pain, sin, or regrets – not things that you've done or not done, not anything others have done to you, not any evil or spiritual opposition – that can diminish God's love for you or stand in the way of His purpose for your life.

God has the last say. He is committed to fulfilling His purpose and calling for you and for me, as we trust Him. There is no global pandemic, war, political corruption, persecution, opposition from other people, or spiritual resistance that can stand against our all-powerful God.

So, rest in His faithfulness. Rest in His promises to fulfill His word and purpose concerning you. Have faith in the One who is greater than every opposition or adversity, the King of kings and Lord of lords, and He will open the floodgates of heaven at just the right time and in just the right way.

Faith releases the promises of God. Faith releases the purposes of God. Most important, faith brings delight to the heart of our heavenly Father.

In every situation, let's rise and declare, God is faithful. He is powerful. He has a purpose, and I can trust His purpose. He is who He says He is, and He will do what He says He will do.

What He has started in you He will complete. What He has started through you he will complete. Greater is He that is in you than he that is in the world. If God is for you, who can be against you?

He **is** working all things together in your life for good. He will perfect that which concerns you. Though heaven and earth shall pass away, his word to you will never pass away. His word is forever settled in the heavens, and His faithfulness endures to all generations.

Thank God for every experience, good and bad, and surrender any unhealed pain and disappointment to Him. Acknowledge His power and desire to work all things together for your good. And trust Him to fulfill His highest purpose in and through you.

God is faithful. Always. Simply believe, trust, and obey – and watch what He will do.

Evaluate

-Describe the top two positive life experiences that most impacted you.

-Describe the top three negative life experiences that had the greatest impact on you.

-How might your life experiences empower you to help others?

Every moment of your life—both the joys and the sorrows—has been woven into the story God is writing through you. Nothing is wasted in His hands. Even the broken places can become altars of grace where His strength shines brightest.

Your past may explain you, but it does not define you; only Christ does. Trust that God is working all things together for good, and let your story become a testimony that points others to His redeeming love.

Each of you should use whatever gift you have received to serve others, as faithful stewards of God's grace in its various forms.[66]

CHAPTER EIGHT
COMBINE THE TOOLS

If you've ever attended a classical concert with a full orchestra, you'll know that the musicians are grouped according to four main sections: the strings, winds, brass, and percussion. Each section is made up of smaller groups. For example, the winds include flutes, clarinets, oboes, and bassoons.

A full-size orchestra will have eighty to a hundred or more musicians, each of whom will be reading their part on sheet music.

The conductor is the master of everything not written on sheet music. Long before the live event, he or she spends hours studying a piece of music and making interpretive decisions about how it should be played to make it as inspiring as possible. The conductor provides expressive and artistic leadership and makes decisions beforehand about the tempo and how it changes as well as the pacing of intensity, subtleties of volume, rhythm, phrasing, and emotional expression. The conductor then teaches the music during rehearsals.

It fills me with joy and amazement to watch and listen to dozens of musicians in a full orchestra playing together as one. Each musician could (and sometimes does) play a lovely solo, but there is something magical about so many musicians and instruments playing together in perfect harmony.

The Orchestra and your Purpose

I like to think of an orchestra as a metaphor for divine purpose. In this metaphor, God is the Master Conductor; the word of God is the sheet music, and the different sections and instruments of an orchestra are the various "purpose tools" we discussed in previous chapters. The musicians, with their diverse gifts, style, and personalities – represent relationships with other believers.

While the focus of this book is helping you discover your individual gifts and calling, you will never reach God's ultimate purpose outside of healthy relationships with others in the Christian community. It's no coincidence that the Bible uses the phrase "body of Christ" to describe the community of believers. We need each other to achieve our purpose. Jesus built a team, and we also need a team – whether you are the leader of a team or a member of a team. We will look at this principle more in *Chapter 12: Overcome Obstacles*.

The most important person in this metaphor is the Orchestra Conductor, representing Jesus. At all times we must keep our focus on Him. As the writer of Hebrews wrote, "... looking unto Jesus, the author and finisher of our faith." [67]

For the remainder of this chapter, you will review and refine your answers to the questions you explored in the previous three chapters. This will help clarify your broad purpose and prepare you to write your mission statement, vision statement, and action plan.

First, gather your answers to the questions from the previous three chapters and read them over. Prayerfully reflect on the answers. Now, choose your top two for each section.

Identify the Top Two

* What are the top two joys, top two sorrows, and top two people groups that you identified in chapter five?

* What are the top two motivational gifts, top two spiritual gifts, and top two talents that you identified in chapter six?

* Describe your personality type.

* What two to three life experiences did you identify in chapter seven as having the greatest impact on you?

Now, read over your responses to the questions listed above. Is it possible to refine one or more of those categories to your top one? If yes, circle your top passion, gift, talent, life experience and people group. If you are not able to narrow it down to your top one, do not pressure yourself to force an answer. Often, more than one gift, passion, and life experience will complement others in fulfilling your calling.

Transform Passion into Purpose

Many people speak or write about "following your passion" or "living your dream" in the context of self-fulfillment. While it is true that living your purpose brings joy and satisfaction, the end goal should not be self-actualization or self-fulfillment. The primary goal must always point to Jesus, with a motivation to honour Him and serve others.

Divine purpose is never about self-centred goals. Any joy and satisfaction you experience are by-products of serving God, not the end goal. Also, serving God will at times include trials, adversity, sacrifice, and suffering– so if your goal is personal happiness, you will not persevere on your pathway of purpose.

Your responses to the questions in this chapter are important purpose-indicators, but they are not enough. You must channel these into solving important needs that God cares deeply about.

The key to realizing a God-inspired dream is to focus on significance, not success; on giving, not receiving. For example, you may have a gift and passion to sing. How can it be transformed into divine purpose? How can it meet a need that God cares deeply about, a need that you also care about? If the motivation of your heart is to achieve fame or material success, you have not identified your divine purpose.

On the other hand, if the motivation of your heart is to bring joy or comfort to people who are lonely, sick, or in despair, or to lead people in worship or lead them to God, you are much closer to identifying your purpose.

Passion is powerful. Gifts are powerful. But when passions and gifts are infused by divine purpose, they are far more powerful. And they will leave a legacy that matters for eternity.

After prayerfully reflecting on your responses to the questions in the previous section, explore these questions:

1. Can you see a pattern or connection in your responses to the various questions? Take time to prayerfully reflect on this. Describe any patterns you see in one or two paragraphs.

2. What are some ways you could use your passion, gifts, and life experience to help the people groups you identified?

Don't rush your responses to these questions. Pray and reflect. Ask God to guide you and remember His promise: "I will instruct you and teach you in the way you should go; I will guide you with my eye."[68]

Experiment

If you are not yet able to provide specific answers to these questions, don't fret. At the very least, you will have a general sense of your passions and gifts. So do something. As Martin Luther King Jr. said, "If you can't fly, then run, if you can't run, then walk, if you can't walk, then crawl, but whatever you do, you have to keep moving forward."

You may have heard the adage, *God can steer a moving vehicle, but He can't move one that is stationary.*

"You have dozens of hidden abilities and gifts you don't know you've got because you've never tried them out," wrote Rick Warren in *The Purpose Driven Life*. "No matter how old you are, I urge you to never stop experimenting."

Be bold and adventurous about exploring, researching, and experimenting. Try something you have never done before. Observe what happens in you. Did that activity leave you drained and unmotivated? Then try something else.

On the other hand, did you feel more alive? Were you inspired with creative ideas and vision? Were you excited? Did your friends or family comment that they had not seen you so motivated about something in a long time?

Did you experience a deep, abiding faith that you were in the centre of God's will? Did that faith remain even when you faced discouragement and seemingly insurmountable obstacles? Did you draw closer to God? Did you feel a deep sense of gratitude to God? Was there a sense of resonating with divine purpose – that you were doing the very thing you were born to do?

If the answer to some of those questions is "yes", then you have begun tapping into your purpose.

Kelsey is an example of someone who identified teaching and writing as her strongest passions and gifts. She also identified that children were the people group she cared about most. But she was uncertain what to do next.

Kelsey wondered if she should write children's books. She explored this possibility by watching a few webinars on writing children's books, then interviewing a children's book author. She tried some writing exercises on topics of interest to children. All these actions helped her realize that writing children's books was *not* part of her calling.

She continued praying, exploring, and exposing herself to new experiences. After several months, she heard of a volunteer opportunity to teach underprivileged immigrant children basic English writing skills and decided to sign up. While teaching her very first class, she felt passion, motivation, and compassion, and realized it was a perfect fit for her. "I just knew this was what God was calling me to do," she says.

Scott is a young man who discovered a passion and gift for helping grieving children by first volunteering to teach in his church's Sunday school. Though he enjoyed teaching the class, he never felt particularly passionate about it, nor did he feel he was making much of a difference. But as he continued with his commitment to teach, he found himself especially drawn to kids who had lost a parent to death or divorce. He spent extra time with these children during the classes.

As he continued to pray, the desire to minister to these children grew. He shared his heart with his pastor, who encouraged him to launch a grief support group for kids. Now, he is not only making a powerful difference in the lives of these children, but he feels he is doing the very thing he was born to do.

Kelsey and Scott may have never discovered their purpose if they had not first experimented with trying new things.

I discovered my vocational passion through a process that took time. Initially my goal was medicine, and I completed two years of the pre-med science program at university. My desire was to eventually practice internal medicine. I loved the sciences, but through discussions with my professors, I learned that my goal would require far more years of training than for a basic MD.

I realized that my passion was not strong enough to invest that much time and money. I took two years off from my education– one year to make money and the second year to travel in Europe. I was not yet a Christian, so prayer was not a part of my process. But when I returned home, I had a strong desire to register in journalism studies. From the very first day of class I knew this was the right fit for me. I loved every one of the courses and graduated with honours.

Ironically, the day after I graduated, a young couple shared the gospel with me (this was the first time anyone had ever shared Christ with me), and I received the Lord. Three days later I started my first job in journalism at a magazine that involved writing at least three articles a month, lots of interviews and travel, and many interesting assignments. Years later I left to freelance for several business magazines.

I loved my career. But in time, God directed me to write books and articles with faith messages, in addition to the speaking and teaching I was already doing. Everything I learned during the years of writing for business magazines prepared me for my ultimate calling in writing and speaking.

My point in telling you this story is: experiment! Be willing to try new things.

Just take one step. If you have a desire to be involved in the business arena, don't sit around and wait for someone to offer you the chairmanship of a Fortune 500 company. Take business courses. Seek out successful businesspeople and get their advice. Learn everything you can and pursue any opportunities that present themselves. Trust God's promise to guide you.

If you have a desire to teach children, teach in your church's Sunday school. Or consider volunteering in a local community project that helps teach life skills to disadvantaged children. Hundreds of non-profit agencies are looking for volunteers.

Perhaps you believe you have a gift to teach the Bible. If so, study scripture. Study some more. Take Bible courses. Listen to recorded messages of spiritually mature speakers. Then, don't turn up your nose when the only opportunities you receive are to teach toddlers in Sunday school.

Experiment. If you truly desire God's will, you can trust him to adjust your direction if you get off track. As you step out to serve others, continually praying for God's guidance, He will give your greater clarity of purpose.

Faith does not mean having all your ducks in a row. It does mean prayerfully taking the next step. Steward what God has revealed to you thus far on your faith journey. Explore your gifts and passions. As you do, those passions will become more clearly defined, and you will develop greater clarity of how they align with your purpose.

Never think your passion or dream is insignificant. If you do whatever God shows you to do; if you are faithful to be the person God created you to be, you will bring great joy to the heart of your heavenly Father. And you will have an eternal impact, whether you realize it in this life or not.

You have been entrusted with God-given passions, talents, abilities, and opportunities. Blended with those are your life experiences that have given you a unique message and mandate to share with the world.

If you do your part to diligently seek to understand, develop, and steward the gifts and opportunities that God provides, He will do His part and lead you each step of the way. As your character develops and you grow in your relationship with Him, God will open doors of opportunity at the right time, in the right way. Read and reflect on Paul's words to the Ephesians 2:10– the Amplified version says it best:

> *For we are His workmanship [His own master work, a work of art], created in Christ Jesus [reborn from above—spiritually transformed, renewed, ready to be used] for good works, which God prepared [for us] beforehand [taking paths which He set], so that we would walk in them.*

You are Father God's precious work of art; He is transforming you, preparing you, and leading you to fulfill the very calling He planned for you before you were born. Trust Him to complete the work He started in you, and through you.

God is faithful—always.

PART III – WRITE

CLARIFY AND WRITE YOUR MISSION STATEMENT, VISION STATEMENT, AND ACTION PLAN

Start writing, no matter what. The water does not flow until the faucet is turned on –
Louis L'Amour, author of ninety-one books.

CHAPTER NINE
WRITE YOUR MISSION STATEMENT

If you've watched the movie, *Apollo 13*, you'll remember the dramatic moment when astronaut Jim Lovell (played by Tom Hanks), uttered these words: *"Houston, we have a problem...."*

If ever there was an understatement, this was it.

The movie is based on the true story of Nasa's Apollo 13 mission. It was supposed to be the third human moon landing. But an explosion two days after the launch derailed that plan. Instead, Apollo 13 became one of the most dramatic, daring, and death-defying adventures in human history. It was an example of the power of global prayer, combined with human ingenuity and courage, triumphing over seemingly impossible odds.

The craft launched from Kennedy Space Centre on April 11th, 1970. At first, everything went according to plan. But just two days into the flight, a catastrophic explosion blew up one oxygen tank. Within moments, the crew realized the second tank was also rapidly leaking oxygen. Next, warning lights indicated the loss of two of three fuel cells, which were the spacecraft's prime source of electricity. There they were, 200 thousand miles from earth, and their command module lost its normal supply of electricity, light, and water.

The astronauts faced the reality they had less than two hours of oxygen; they could be poisoned by carbon dioxide accumulations, and they could freeze to death. Even if they managed to return to the earth's atmosphere, they had to enter at precisely the right angle, or they would burn up and evaporate. And they had to somehow do that with no navigational equipment.

From a human perspective, it was an impossible task. So how did they do it? While many decisions and actions contributed to Apollo 13's successful landing, two things were paramount: 1) clear mission, and 2) global prayer.

The mission? Get the astronauts back to earth safely. To do that, Nasa engineers and ground controllers at Mission Control in Houston had to write completely new procedures, which had to be tested in a simulator. And they had to design those procedures using only the materials that were still available on the Apollo 13 spacecraft.

As Flight Director Gene Kranz famously said, "I don't

care what anything was DESIGNED to do, I care about what it CAN do."

Teams of flight controllers at Mission Control, supported by thousands of engineers across America, worked around the clock for four days to try and give the astronauts a fighting chance.

As the hours and days progressed, the situation looked increasingly hopeless. But when the Nasa Director said, "This could be the worst disaster NASA's ever experienced," Gene Kranz replied, "With all due respect, sir, I believe this is going to be our finest hour."

Kranz was right. Many called their successful landing a miracle.

Nasa engineer Jerry Woodfill, who was working at his console at Johnson Space Centre as the drama unfolded, later said: "Without divine intervention, the crew and Johnson Space Centre's mission control team could not have overcome the obstacles and brought the astronauts home safely."

Millions of people around the world covered the astronauts and Mission Control engineers in prayer. Thousands prayed in New York City's Times Square, at Chicago's board of trade, at the Wailing Wall in Jerusalem, and in St. Peter's Square where the pope led fifty thousand people in prayer for the astronauts' safe return.

The Senate and House passed resolutions asking all Americans to pray. President Nixon called the nation to a Day of Prayer. Special services and masses were held in tens of thousands of churches and synagogues around the world.

Finally on April 17th, 1970, the crew landed successfully. Prayer and a focused, clear mission were essential to Apollo 13's success.

Prayer and a focused mission are equally essential to fulfilling your personal calling. Throughout this book I have emphasized the spiritual aspects of fulfilling your purpose, including prayer.

In this chapter, we will discuss the importance of a clear mission, and the characteristics of effective mission statements.

Why You Need a Personal Mission Statement

The late Zig Ziglar said, "Outstanding people have one thing in common: An absolute sense of mission." Ziglar was a popular motivational speaker and the author of twenty-eight books, including ten bestsellers.

That's easier said than done. In today's technology-filled world, it's harder than ever to focus. With distractions coming from phone and app notifications, never-ending emails, and ever-expanding social media platforms, focus doesn't come naturally. We must work at it.

Several years ago, I attended a seminar where the attendees were asked to define their personal mission, or corporate mission, in one sentence. Out of a group of about three hundred people, fewer than a dozen were able to articulate a mission statement.

Why does writing a mission statement seem like such a daunting task to so many?

I believe the main reason is a lack of practical resources. Though you can avail yourself of a plethora of advice about mission statements from management experts, books, and the Internet – most of this information is complex and confusing. And most of these resources apply mainly to large corporations and organizations, providing little practical advice for an individual who wants to craft a personal mission statement.

Benefits of a Personal Mission Statement

Even if you lead a corporation, small business, non-profit, or ministry, writing a personal mission statement should be done first before writing one for your organization.

Why? It will help you evaluate whether your current occupation, ministry, or organization aligns with your calling. It will help you answer crucial questions like these:

- Does my current occupation align with my personal calling?
- If not, are there changes I can make in my role/ responsibilities to bring my occupation more in line with my calling? What are those changes?
- If changes are not an option, are there other benefits to remaining in my current occupation that will help prepare and equip me to fulfill my mission in the future? Am I developing skills or learning lessons that will be of future benefit?
  For example, you may have a passion to launch a non-profit that provides job skills training to mentally challenged teens. Your current occupation involves bookkeeping

and administration for a multi-national corporation – an occupation that you find tedious and boring. However, you may be learning vital skills that will be necessary when leading your own non-profit.

- If there are no benefits to remaining in my current occupation, do I need to identify an entirely new direction? If so, how can I prepare?
- Should I lead my own vision, or should I join another vision? One of the greatest benefits of writing a personal mission statement is it will help you identify a ministry or organization that is a good fit for your gifts, passions, and mission. Some people think that writing a personal mission statement applies only to people who want to start and lead a new ministry, organization, or business. Some people are called to lead a vision, but most are not. Most will find their highest purpose serving under another vision. Writing a personal mission statement will help you identify who you want to partner with, and how you might best serve with that organization's vision.

Your personal mission statement is the benchmark for answering all those questions.

"A mission statement becomes the DNA for every other decision we will make," said Stephen Covey, renowned leadership expert and best-selling author of many books, including the popular *7 Habits of Highly Successful People*. "All the goals and decisions you will make in the future will be based upon it."

A mission statement makes a general idea or dream specific. This takes work. It's not good enough to have vague ideas, passions, and dreams. You must write them down. The writing process will:

- Clarify your mission or dream
- Establish focus
- Motivate and inspire you
- Define your priorities
- Propel you to take action
- Keep you accountable for how you invest your time, talents, and resources

The simple act of writing your vision is a powerful catalyst for launching you into your destiny. As the prophet Habakkuk wrote, "Write the vision and make it plain on tablets, that he many run who reads it."[69]

Does writing a mission statement limit God?

Are you worried that defining your mission will limit God? Or are you afraid you won't get it right?

Time and again people will say they are afraid of misinterpreting God's will. They say things like, "How can I be sure I'm accurately discerning God's purposes? Isn't it presumptuous to write out my own plan? How does planning allow for divine intervention?"

As already discussed in chapter four, purpose is path that is walked one step at a time. We can only define our mission based on the revelation we have received at this point on our spiritual journey.

Over time, your mission statement may become more refined. As you grow in your relationship with God, revelation of your calling will also become more specific and focused. This does not mean your purpose has completely changed; it simply means that you have acquired clearer revelation of your purpose.

In other words, your mission statement is not written in stone. You can and should revisit it periodically. Most likely you will revise and fine-tune it time and again. Don't be concerned about whether it is precisely accurate. Trust the Holy Spirit to lead you in this endeavour.

God wants us to plan, but don't worry! He will override any plan that doesn't conform to His sovereign will. This is why it is vital we do not clutch our list of goals as if they were written in permanent marker.

I trust that as I spend regular time with God to seek His wisdom, He will direct my steps, or re-direct my steps when necessary. The scriptures promise that the Holy Spirit will guide me into all truth, and instruct me and teach me in the way I should go.[70]

What is a mission statement?

Type "mission statement definition" in Google and you'll get 650 million plus results. While there are many different opinions, in recent years, most management experts have come to agree that the best mission statements represent a simple, concise description of broad purpose that does not include specific initiatives, strategies, or goals.

Before we discuss the elements of an effective mission statement, I want to provide some simple definitions:

Mission Statement: A mission statement is present-oriented. It is a brief statement of fundamental purpose that answers these questions: *What is my purpose? What do I do? Why do I do what I do? And for whom?* For an organization it answers the question, *What is the fundamental purpose of the organization?*

Vision Statement: A vision statement is future-oriented and describes what a person or organization would like to achieve in the mid to long-term future. It represents the future results of accomplishing your mission or purpose. (Note, throughout this book, I use the terms *mission* and *purpose* interchangeably).

Core Values: Core values are the fundamental beliefs and principles that guide an individual or organization. Personal core values play an important role in guiding the goals you set. For Christians, the scriptures should be the moral basis for setting personal core values.

Goal: A description of *what* you want to achieve, including tangible ways you will accomplish your mission and ultimately reach your vision. Goals can be short-term or long-term and they must be specific, measurable, and time bound (see chapter twelve).

Action Plan: Specific details about how to achieve your goals. The plan includes specific action steps to achieve your goals, including deadlines. Action plans are flexible and open to change as needed.

Elements of Effective Mission Statements

First, let's talk about what a mission statement is **not**.

A mission statement is *not* a job description, role, or specific assignment. It is *not* a to-do list or statement of goals. It is *not* a strategic plan.

Your mission defines your broad purpose. Purpose is

the *why* – the reason you do what you do (or what you desire to do). It states what you believe God has called you to do as you understand it at this time. It briefly answers the questions: *What*? And *Why*? – preferably in one sentence.

The answer to these questions must be broad enough to encompass many activities and roles throughout your life. You write it as though it will never change. It could change as you mature and grow in your relationship with God, but it should be written as though it is timeless.

Following are elements of an effective mission statement:

- It must be clear, focused, and brief.
- It must be inspiring to you, since you are the one who will be carrying out the mission. It must not be written to impress others; it needs to inspire you.
- It will be specific to you and your unique passions, gifts, and strengths.
- It should be timeless. You write it as though it will never change, although as previously said, it may change as you continue to mature spiritually.
- It must be easy to remember.
- You should be able to define it in one concise sentence – two sentences at most.

Mission Statement Examples

Before writing my personal mission statement, I found it helpful to read mission statements for successful companies, ministries, and individuals. I believe these examples will also help you to understand how to write an effective mission statement.

Note: Numerous additional mission statement examples, as well as step-by-step guidance in crafting a personal mission and vision statement, are provided in my free e-book, Write Your Personal Mission & Vision Statements. A link is provided at the end of this chapter. Also, if you do not have time to work on your mission statement, I suggest you skip the rest of this chapter and avail yourself to my free e-book when you can set aside the time.

Corporate Mission Statement Examples

Google: to organize the world's information and make it universally accessible and useful.

As you know, at one time Google was a search engine, nothing more, nothing less. But the company expanded into many other activities. However, Google's mission statement today is the same as when it was just a search engine. This exemplifies the importance of a mission statement being broad enough to grow with you or your company, and encompass many different strategies, goals, and activities that accompany that growth.

Meta: Build the future of human connection and the technology that makes it possible. (Meta owns Facebook, Instagram, Messenger, Threads, and WhatsApp.)

Amazon: To be earth's most customer centric company; to build a place where people can come to find and discover anything they might want to buy online.

Apple: To bring the best personal computing products and support to students, educators, designers, scientists, engineers, businesspersons, and consumers in over 140 countries around the world.

LinkedIn: Connect the world's professionals to make them more productive and successful.

Microsoft: Microsoft's mission statement has evolved over the years, reflecting the rapid changes in technology. Currently it reads: Our mission is to empower every person and every organization on the planet to achieve more.

Tesla: To accelerate the world's transition to sustainable energy.

Ministry Mission Statement Examples

The Global Leadership Network: To inspire and equip world-class leadership that ignites transformation.

Mother Teresa: To serve Christ by ministering to the poor, the dying, and the hopelessly ill wherever the needy cried out for help.

Victory Churches International: Reach every available person, at every available time, with every available means, with the life changing gospel of our Lord Jesus Christ.

Women Together: To engage Canadian Christian women to provide education, leadership training, skills development, and Biblical instruction to women leaders around the world.

Wycliffe Bible Translators: Ending Bible poverty by facilitating the translation of God's Word among minority language communities worldwide.

Personal Mission Statement Examples

Franklin Roosevelt: To end the Depression.

Andrew Carnegie (who at one time was the richest man in the world): To spend the first half of my life making as much money as I can – and the second half giving it away. (He gave away 90 percent of his fortune).

Jack Canfield, co-author of the outrageously successful *Chicken Soup for the Soul* book series: To empower people to live their highest vision in a context of love and joy.

John C. Maxwell: author, speaker, and pastor who has written many best-selling books on leadership: Growing and equipping others to do remarkable things and lead significant and fulfilled lives.

Briefly Describe Main Activities

After writing your one-sentence mission statement, write the main activities that will help you achieve your mission. At this point you are not writing specific goals or strategies; you are simply listing the main activities involved in your mission. You are briefly answering the question, in general terms, ***How** will I accomplish my mission?*

Many people find it easier to write their one-sentence personal mission statement *after* first identifying their main activities. That is the process I used in developing my mission statement.

After defining my passions, gifts, strengths, and the activities that gave me a sense of purpose, I summarized them as follows:

- Writing books and e-books

- Speaking at conferences, retreats, and churches
- Conducting seminars and webinars
- Teaching with online tools, such as YouTube and Zoom

The people group I desired to help are those who long to become all that God has created them to be, and to do what He has called them to do.

To create my one-sentence mission statement, I asked myself: *Why* do I write and speak? How can my writing and speaking help others, and fulfill a need that God cares deeply about? I took my time with this process and wrote lots of possible mission statements, until I clarified it as follows:

To equip and empower others to fulfill their divine purpose.

That is my *why*. I love to see people set free from inner prisons, self-doubt, and fears to become all that God created them to be, and to fulfill their divine purpose.

Many others could have a similar mission statement to me, but different strategies (main activities) reflecting their unique passions and gifts. To summarize, here is my mission statement followed by my main activities:

Judy Rushfeldt Mission: *To equip and empower others to fulfill their divine purpose.*

This will be accomplished by:

- Writing books, e-books and articles
- Speaking at conferences, retreats, and churches
- Conducting seminars and webinars
- Teaching with online tools

The main activities have evolved over time and may

evolve more in the future. But my one-sentence mission statement remains the same.

I highly recommend this format (one-sentence mission statement plus brief list of main activities) for individuals, as well as smaller companies, churches, ministries, and organizations. Why? It helps you focus on your priorities. The first statement is what motivates and inspires you. The main activities help you focus. That's especially important if you are a creative person who gets so many ideas that you are easily distracted.

This format is not as important for large companies, because they have dozens of divisions and hundreds of executive level staff in place to identify strategies for each division. With that said, some of the most successful large companies, like Meta, use this format.

As you read through these examples, you will notice that the activities are not a complete list of everything the organizations do – just broad descriptions of overarching, main activities. Ideally there should be three to five brief statements of main activities, or one paragraph, and no more. Following are a few examples.

Meta

Mission statement: Build the future of human connection and the technology that makes it possible.

Main activities (described as "mission objectives"):

- Expand digital connectivity infrastructure
- Enhance user engagement across platforms
- Develop advanced communication technologies

Homes for Heroes

Mission statement: To integrate all our homeless military veterans into the community through the provision of housing and support services across Canada.

Main Activities:

- Build unique and affordable urban villages in major cities across Canada where homeless veterans will be able to successfully integrate back into civilian life
- Provide the resources, services and training they will need to achieve the goal of living independently in the long term

Team Leadership College International (TLCI)

Mission: Equip ordinary people to become victorious leaders who affect change in every arena of society: in their home, local church, community, marketplace, and nation.

Main activities:

- Biblical teaching from proven, successful, spiritual Christian pastors and leaders from more than 18 different countries
- Front lines ministry and missions training
- Intentional and focused mentorship of the students by seasoned leaders. (My husband and I regularly teach courses on Zoom for TLCI, and we love their ministry and students).

Jack Canfield

Mission: To empower people to live their highest vision in a context of love and joy.

Main activities: We do this by delivering excellent content and training that expands awareness, builds self-confidence, fosters cooperation, reduces hatred and intolerance, improves relationships, and empowers individuals and organizations to achieve their goals and dreams.

Similar gifts, different missions

You may have a similar gift as someone else, but a completely different passion and mission. You are God's unique work of art. Just as He did not make two snowflakes alike, He did not make two people alike. Let's look at an example of two individuals with similar gifts, but different passions and missions.

What are their gifts? Both gentlemen have the gifts to lead people, grow successful businesses, and make lots of money. But they have different passions that make their missions unique. One of these individuals has a passion to help underprivileged children in developing countries. The other has a passion to mentor young men in his employ.

The first man, who has a passion for impoverished children, partners with Compassion International, which provides food, clothing, education, and spiritual support to children in impoverished countries. The last I heard, this gentleman was sponsoring over one hundred children, all in the same region in Africa. Not only does he support them financially, but every year he spends several weeks in the area ministering to those kids and their families.

If I were asked to develop a mission statement for him, I would write something like this:

Mission: To serve impoverished children in developing countries by providing for their physical, educational, emotional, and spiritual needs.

Then I would write the main activities, which could look something like this:

- Build my business to increase wealth
- Increase the number of children I support
- Visit Africa periodically to provide personal support and encouragement to the children and their families

Let's look at the second gentleman, whose passion is to mentor young men. He owns a successful oil service company in western Canada with about three hundred employees. The employees, most of whom are young men, work in oilfields away from their families and communities for weeks at a time.

This gentleman makes lots of money, but for him, it's not about the money. The money is a tool to help fulfill his passion to mentor and minister to the young men in his employ.

How does he do that? He meets regularly with each of his employees, not only to discuss the job, but to encourage them in their personal lives. He asks how they are doing. He asks how their families are doing.

He demonstrates his care and concern in many personal and practical ways. In time, as trust is developed, most of the employees open up and talk about personal issues, family problems, and other concerns. He gives advice and encouragement. He offers to pray for them. When appropriate, he arranges for practical support and resources for their families.

So here you have three hundred employees, many of

whom would never go to a church, having a direct encounter with God through the prayers and practical actions of this man's pastoral marketplace ministry. As a result, many have opened their hearts to Christ. If I were asked to write a mission statement for this gentleman, it would say something like this:

Mission: To mentor, pastor, and serve young men.

For main activities, I would write:

- Build greater wealth for philanthropic purposes
- Meet regularly with each employee to provide mentoring and pastoral support
- Provide practical resources to help the young men and their families

Do you see how individuals with similar passions and gifts can have very different missions?

The Writing Process

It's time. Time to get out your notepad, tablet, or desktop – and begin writing.

This is where many people stall. *I don't feel ready*, you may be thinking. Or, *what if I get it wrong?* Or, *this is important, and I want to be sure of my mission before I put anything on paper. I don't want to mess it up.*

You very well might get it wrong. But you'll never get it right until you start writing. I always encourage people to write several possible mission statements. The more you write, the clearer it will become.

As theologian, author, and pastor George Herbert said: "Do not wait; the time will never be *just right.* Start where you stand, and work with whatever tools you may have at your command, and better tools will be found as you go along."

Schedule at least a couple of hours to write your first draft. I recommend you set your notes aside for a week or two. Then spend another hour or so revising, refining, and adding new thoughts. At that point, you may be able to complete your mission statement and main activities. On the other hand, you may need several more sessions. It doesn't matter how long it takes; be patient with the process.

Give yourself permission to dream. Take whatever time you need to prayerfully explore your passions, purpose, and the people groups you care about. As already mentioned, your first efforts are a draft, not the final product. Don't try and get it perfect in the initial stages of writing. Take lots of time for prayer and reflection.

For step-by-step guidance in writing your mission and vision statements, I would like to offer you my free e-book: Write Your Personal Mission & Vision Statements. This e-book includes much more material than can be included in this chapter. Click on this link to access:
JudyRushfeldt.com

Your mission statement is more than words on a page —it's the compass that points you toward your God-given destiny. It will remind you who you are, why you are here, and what matters most when distractions, disappointments, or doubts arise.

A clear mission statement will not only inspire you but also keep you moving forward when the journey gets hard. It will simplify your decisions, sharpen your priorities, and strengthen your faith.

Remember, God doesn't need polished words—He desires a surrendered heart. Don't wait for perfect clarity; start writing, praying, refining, and living it today. As you do, you'll be amazed at how God breathes purpose into every part of your life.

Most importantly, hold your mission statement with open hands, allowing God to refine it as He leads you into new seasons. A mission statement is not meant to confine you, but to propel you into the purposeful life God has planned.

Everyone has his own specific vocation or mission in life...Therein he cannot be replaced, nor can his life be repeated, thus, everyone's task is unique as his specific opportunity to implement it

- Viktor E. Frankl

In the long run men only hit what they aim for – Henry David Thoreau

CHAPTER TEN
WRITE YOUR VISION STATEMENT

Can you imagine a world with no Micky Mouse, Snow White, or Sleeping Beauty? No Belle, Simba, or Bambi? No Donald Duck, Elsa, or Olaf? Considered one of modern history's greatest visionaries, Walt Disney impacted the lives of children (and adults) all around the world. His motto was: *Dream, Believe, Dare, Do*.

Disney was a Christian who stated: "Whatever success I have had in bringing clean, informative entertainment to people of all ages, I attribute in great part to my Congregational upbringing and my lifelong habit of prayer."

"I dream," Disney said. "I test my dreams against my beliefs, I dare to take risks, and I execute my vision to make those dreams come true."

Historian and author Jim Korkis tells this story about Disney's visionary imagination:

> As Walt Disney stood on the marshy central Florida land in the heat and humidity, he did not see an inhospitable landscape with dangerous swamps hidden in thick forests of tangled trees and scrub brush.
>
> As he shaded his eyes and squinted into the flat horizon, Walt saw clearly a bright city of tomorrow, families enjoying themselves, a towering castle, innovative hotels that were themed and much, much more.[71]

Vision is futuristic. Walt's Disney's vision for that piece of land in Florida focused on its future potential, not the dismal, challenging terrain of the present.

Your mission statement describes your purpose – the *why* of what you do or what you want to do. Your vision statement, on the other hand, describes the potential future results of you fulfilling your mission. It paints a clear, specific, compelling picture of what the future would look like if you accomplished your mission.

Your vision statement should answer the questions: *What impact or change do I envision could occur if I accomplish my mission? What could the future look like if I fulfill my purpose?* For an organization, it also answers the question: *Where does the organization want to be in five or ten years? What is the organization working towards achieving?*

To explore and define your vision statement, you will need to let go of the adult tendency to dream small dreams and instead embrace the possibility-thinking of a child.

Ask a group of five-year-olds what they want to be when they grow up and they'll say things like, "I want to be . . . a fireman . . . an author . . . a lawyer . . . a world traveller . . . the first female president of the United States . . . a mom . . . an artist . . . a missionary . . . a foster parent . . . a pilot . . . an evangelist . . . the founder of an orphanage . . . the president of the world's biggest company . . ."

Watch how their eyes sparkle with enthusiasm as they share their dreams. Their attitude seems to say, "I can do anything. The opportunities are endless. The world is my footstool."

Dreaming is natural for most children, for life has not yet hardened their hearts. They remain attuned to that visionary trait that God carves into the soul of every human being. But somewhere along the sojourn from childhood to adulthood, many of us disengage from our inner dreamer.

To freely dream, we must not limit our vision to what we can accomplish through human effort alone. As George Barna wrote in *The Power of Vision*: "While individuals may dream big, they also will dream realistically...those visions are based upon the ability of the human mind to conceive a grand plan. Without supernatural intervention, we cannot dream any bigger than our imagination will allow." [72]

Instead, allow your spirit to imagine your potential through God. As Jesus said, "With people it is impossible, but not with God; for with God all things are possible."[73]

Choose now to open your heart and spirit to what God

could do through you as you live out your divine purpose and calling.

Why you should define your vision:

- It produces focus and helps you establish priorities.
- It provides motivation and inspiration.
- It helps guide decision-making.
- It attracts others.
- It motivates you to accomplish your goals.
- It helps you persevere towards your dream when you encounter adversity and opposition.
- For corporations, organizations, and ministries, it also acts as a unifying force, helps guide employees, and improves overall organizational effectiveness.

Another important benefit of a vision statement for individuals is it will help you determine whether you should lead a vision or join another vision that reflects your own passion.

"If you want to accomplish a dream," wrote John Maxwell, "you will be able to do so only when you can see it clearly."

Elements of an Effective Vision Statement

A vision statement is not a detailed plan; rather it inspires and guides actions. It must not be vague, complicated, or boring. An effective vision statement has the following characteristics:

- It is clear, focused, inspiring, and brief enough to remember.

- It paints a vivid and motivating picture of the mid-to-long-term future (for example, five to ten years in the future).
- It is so big that it is compelling.
- It conveys passion.
- It evokes hope. It creates growing anticipation for the future.
- It should answer these questions: *Where do I want to go? What is the end result that I am hoping and praying for? What impact do I want to have? What legacy do I want to leave?*
- Ideally, it should be stated in the present tense, as if it has already happened. Although it relates to the future, it must be grounded in the present.

Let's look at some examples.(Many additional examples are provided in my free e-book: Write Your Personal Mission & Vision Statements. A link is provided at the end of the chapter.)

Organizational Vision Statement Examples

Let's look at some examples of effective vision statements that meet the above criteria. This will help when you write your own vision statement.

Homes for Heroes: End homelessness amongst Canadian military veterans.

Oxfam: A just world without poverty

Meta: To bring the metaverse to life and help people connect, find communities and grow businesses.

Google: To provide access to the world's information in one click.

The Alzheimer's Association: A world without Alzheimer's.

Saddleback Church (Lake Forest, CA): A place where the hurting, the depressed, the frustrated, and the confused find love, acceptance, help, hope, forgiveness, guidance, and encouragement.

Compassion International: Releasing children from poverty in Jesus' name.

Personal Vision Statement Examples

Tony Robbins (best-selling author): Empowering individuals and organizations to make a significant difference in their quality of life and the lives of others.

Joni Eareckson Tada (author, speaker, and a quadriplegic who is a respected global leader in disability advocacy): A world where every person with a disability finds hope, dignity, and their place in the body of Christ.

Mission plus Vision Examples

In the following examples, I will combine vision statements with the mission statements, to help show the differences between mission and vision.

Meta (Facebook)
Mission statement: to give people the power to share and make the world more open and connected.
Vision statement: To bring the metaverse to life and help people connect, find communities and grow businesses.

Google
Mission statement: To organize the world's information and make it universally accessible and useful.
Vision statement: To provide access to the world's

information in one click.

LinkedIn

Mission statement: Connect the world's professionals to make them more productive and successful.
Vision statement: Create economic opportunity for every member of the global workforce.

Apple

Mission statement: To bring the best personal computing products and support to students, educators, designers, scientists, engineers, businesspersons, and consumers in over 140 countries around the world.
Vision statement: To make the best products on earth and to leave the world better than we found it.

The Salvation Army

Mission statement: The Salvation Army exists to share the love of Jesus Christ, meet human needs and be a transforming influence in the community of our world.
Vision statement: We are an innovative partner, mobilized to share hope wherever there is hardship, building communities that are just and know the love of Jesus.

Disney

Mission statement: To entertain, inform and inspire people around the globe through the power of unparalleled storytelling, reflecting the iconic brands, creative minds and innovative technologies that make ours the world's premier entertainment company.
Vision statement: To be one of the world's leading producers and providers of entertainment and information.

Anonymous personal vision statements:

- Everyone in my city is healthy and happy.
- The whole world is coming to me to hear my advice on issues I am qualified to speak on.
- A world free of animal cruelty.
- Everyone in my community has heard the gospel of Jesus Christ.
- A world where everyone is living to their full potential.
- I am solving challenging problems in the field of nuclear energy.

Write Your Vision Statement

Now it's time to write your own vision statement. Take your time with this. Writing a vision statement (as well as a mission statement) is a process, so don't rush your responses.

Start by picturing in your mind the people group you identified that you would like to help. What is the end result you hope to see happen in their lives as a result of you fulfilling your mission?

Ask yourself, *What do I desire that God will do in and through their lives, as a result of me accomplishing my mission?*

I like what David Jeremiah, author, pastor, and founder of Turning Point Radio and Television Ministries said: "The only way the corporate Body of Christ will fulfill the mission Christ has given it is for individual Christians to have a vision for fulfilling that mission."

Remember, your vision statement is a concise, specific statement of the potential end result of accomplishing your divine mission. An effective vision statement will serve as a compass to keep things going in the right direction. It will help you measure your progress, set goals, establish priorities, and know when to use one of the most important words in your vocabulary: *No*.

Vision Boards

Are you a visual person? Do images inspire you and help you visualize the future you want? You may find it beneficial to create a vision board. A vision board is a visual representation of your vision statement. It is a collection of images and words that inspire you to reach your goals.

A vision board can be physical or digital. You can create it on a poster, a piece of paper, a page in your journal, or digitally.

If you create your vision board digitally, there are lots of free apps like Canva available online. The benefit of a digital vision board is that you will have access to millions of images that represent your vision.

Typically, a vision board consists of images, photos, and scriptures, quotes, or affirmations. For example, let's say your five-year vision is to be debt-free and own your own home. Your vision board could have pictures of your dream home, quotes about financial freedom, and scriptures about God's provision. You could include pictures of you and your family on a beach, representing a dream vacation that you would take after you are debt-free.

The Internet has lots of resources to help you in creating a vision board. The only limit to your vision board is your imagination.

For step-by-step guidance in writing your mission and

vision statements, I would like to offer you my free e-book: Write Your Personal Mission & Vision Statements. This e-book includes much more material than can be included in this chapter. Click on this link to access:
JudyRushfeldt.com

Crafting a vision statement is a powerful exercise that can shape the path of your mission. By clearly articulating your vision, you create a roadmap that guides your decisions, actions, and priorities. A well-defined vision statement not only inspires you but also motivates others to join your vision. It serves as a constant reminder of the future you aspire to create and the impact you wish to have in your arena of influence.

Remember, your vision statement should be clear, concise, and compelling. It should paint a vivid picture of the future, evoke passion, and instill hope. As you write your vision statement, focus on the people you want to help and the change you want to bring about. Let it be a reflection of your deepest aspirations and your commitment to making a difference.

Embrace the power of vision and let it propel you towards a future filled with purpose, passion, and possibility.

Dreams don't work unless you do —John C. Maxwell.

CHAPTER ELEVEN
DEVELOP YOUR ACTION PLAN

You've defined your mission and vision statements. Now what?

It's time to transform purpose into action. Dreams without action are just that – dreams. Anyone can dream, but no dream ever comes true unless you are willing to wake up and go to work.

Mission and vision statements provide clarity, inspiration, and focus to your passions and dreams. An action plan involves setting specific goals for accomplishing your dream. With no goals, your mission and vision statements will go no further than the paper or device where you wrote them. Think of your goals as tools for achieving your purpose.

"Without goals, and plans to reach them, you are like a ship that has set sail with no destination," wrote author, psychologist, and pastor Fitzhugh Dodson.

A recent study found that 92 percent of people who set New Year's goals never achieve them. Of the eight percent that do reach their goals, a major factor in their success was writing a plan that included specific goals as well as a roadmap to reach those goals.

If you don't like planning, you're not alone. Neither do I. And neither do most people. After all, planning takes time, discipline, focus, and determination.

Excuses for Not Planning

We all have different reasons and excuses for not planning. Here are the most common:

- It's a waste of time. Many people equate productivity with busyness, not realizing how much time they waste on unimportant activities because they didn't set priorities and goals.
- Planning requires decisiveness. Some people love making decisions, but many people find decision-making to be exhausting.
- Planning is hard work.
- Some people fear they will not clearly discern God's will in their plan, so they do nothing.
- Planning requires commitment and discipline.
- A plan might be outdated by the time it is completed. That's true – circumstances change and a plan must be flexible.

I like something best-selling author Stephen Covey wrote:

> Before taking off, a pilot has a very clear destination in mind. The plane takes off toward that predetermined

destination. But in fact, the plane is off course at least 90 percent of the time. Weather conditions, turbulence, and other factors cause it to get off track. However, feedback is given to the pilot constantly, who then makes course corrections and keeps coming back to the exact flight plan, bringing the plane back on course. ....Amazing – leaving on time, often arriving on time, but off course 90 percent of the time.[74]

Does planning limit God?

Some Christians believe it's wrong to plan. They believe it is presumptuous, or they think it hinders the leading of the Holy Spirit.

It's true that a plan can limit God if not kept in the right perspective. Your plan must be flexible. It must be prepared prayerfully. And you must be open to God changing that plan at any moment. You've likely heard it said, "Write your plans in pencil, and give God the eraser and pen."

Your plan is a tool for taking steps toward the dream God planted in your heart. It is a tool – no more, no less. You don't serve the tool or the plan; you serve God, and the plan serves you. It's important to review your plan periodically and prayerfully. It's equally important to pray each day that God will order your footsteps and direct your pathways.

I can think of many times that I had a plan for my day, but the Holy Spirit re-directed me. Other times, circumstances re-directed me. A friend or family member was hurting and needed my help, or a crisis developed that needed my attention.

During the last several years of my parents' lives, they

were in rapidly deteriorating health; both had dementia, both were in wheelchairs, and I was their primary caregiver. Those of you who have cared for elderly parents with high medical needs will know how rapidly, frequently, and unexpectedly their health can change. But because family is a core value for me, I accepted that my personal plans would be constantly interrupted. And that's okay. I loved them deeply and they deserved the best of care.

Another season of life when my plans came to a sudden halt was when I was seriously injured in a car accident, after a speeding truck jumped the median and hit me head on. Between the pain of a major burst spinal fracture, multiple soft tissue injuries, and a severe concussion, I was no longer physically or mentally capable of writing or speaking. I could barely read, and was unable to walk more than a few steps for several months. It took several years for me to regain my health. I had to come to a place of accepting that my dreams were on pause, which was very difficult for a vision and task-oriented person like me.

I'm sure that most of you have also had to adapt to seasons of adversity and hardship – at least, those of you who have lived long enough.

Just because your plans need to be flexible and open to change does not mean you shouldn't plan. Humility and sensitivity to the Holy Spirit are key. Don't run ahead of God, but don't lag behind either. Act in faith according to your understanding of God's purpose at each stage of your spiritual journey.

If you keep your heart humble, stay focused on Jesus, and continually seek His direction, you can trust Him to adjust or revise or completely change your plans if you get off track. As the writer of Proverbs said, “A man’s heart plans his way, but the Lord directs his steps.”[75]

Benefits of a Plan

Goals put feet to your vision. You may have great dreams and vision, but if you do not translate that vision into tangible goals, you will never see any results. Many people go through life accomplishing nothing because they never set goals. They may talk to anyone who will listen about their wonderful vision, exciting dreams, creative ideas, and grandiose plans—but they spend their life running around in circles, expending huge amounts of energy, but never going anywhere.

“Setting and achieving goals is one of the best ways to measure your life’s progress and create unusual clarity,” wrote Jack Canfield, Mark Victor Hansen, and Les Hewitt. “Consider the alternative—just drifting along aimlessly, hoping that one day good fortune will fall into your lap with little or no effort on your part. Wake up! You’ve got more chance of finding a grain of sugar on a sandy beach.”[76]

When you consider the size of your dream, do you feel so overwhelmed that you struggle to get started? Here are some benefits of planning:

- It breaks down a big dream into smaller, manageable pieces. This will go a long way towards reducing stress and anxiety.
- A plan helps you set wise goals.
- It will help you establish priorities and identify which tasks should be tackled first.
- Your plan will help you manage your time more

efficiently.

- Planning helps you make decisions about how to allocate resources (including staff, if applicable).
- Planning leads to action.

How many people do you know that you've heard say, *I want to write a book; I want to learn an instrument; I want to start my own business; I want to spend a summer volunteering with an orphanage in Africa....someday*. And in many, if not most cases, someday never arrives.

In just the last couple of years, three people have told me they want to write a book and asked my advice. I typically provide one or two simple steps for getting started to see how serious they are. Not one person has followed through. The reality is that many people want to *have written* a book. But most do not want to invest the hard work and discipline involved in the writing process.

Dreams without action are simply fantasies or daydreams. Any kind of planning is better than no plan at all. As Yogi Berra said, "If you don't know where you are going, you'll end up someplace else."

What is your greatest practical resource? Money? Talent? Connections? I believe our greatest practical resource is none of those. It's time. We all have the same amount: 1440 minutes each day. To steward that resource, you need a planner.

"Do you love life?" asks Benjamin Franklin. "Then do not squander time, for time is the stuff that life is made of."

You can start by planning your week, then a month, then a year. Once you write longer term plans, you can be sure they will change, and that's fine. God opens new doors or closes doors that are not the best for you. Or He may redirect you as you continue in prayer.

And of course, life happens. Circumstances change. Personal and family issues arise that require your time and energy. Just like the pilot whose plan gets off course as a result of weather conditions and turbulence, things will happen that require you to update your plan. But any kind of planning is better than no plan.

Start by saying "No"

The first step to planning is to decide what you are willing to NOT do.

Consider the words of the apostle Paul:

> *Brethren, I do not count myself to have apprehended; but one thing I do, forgetting those things which are behind and reaching forward to those things which are ahead, I press toward the goal for the prize of the upward call of God in Christ Jesus.*[77]

If you want to reach your dream, the first step is usually to quit something. End something. Say no to something that is draining far too much of your time and energy.

I've heard people say, "I don't have time to pursue a dream." Yet those same people spend endless hours on social media, watching the news or sports or Netflix, or online shopping. There's nothing wrong with any of those things; we all need hobbies, fun, and recreation. But if you spend too much time on them, they could cost you your dream.

No doubt you have heard of multi-billionaire Warren

Buffet, one of the world's most successful investors. "The difference between successful people and really successful people," he said, "is that really successful people say *no* to almost everything."

You have a finite amount of time, energy, talent, passion, money, and other resources. Embracing the new things God wants to do in and through you will require ending those things that are draining too much of your time and energy.

How do you do that? Unless you are one of those rare individuals who has a lot of free time on your hands, you will need to end something. Quit something. Say no to something that is keeping you from focusing on those things you do best – those things God has called you to do.

This is especially true of leaders. By its very nature, leadership challenges you to continually hone your skills, abilities, and talents. The more you mature and grow as a leader, the more skilled you will become at managing a variety of tasks and responsibilities.

Successful people can do many things well. But by diffusing your time, energy, and talents into many different tasks, you will have limited resources to devote to those few things you are uniquely gifted and called to do.

This is also true of businesses. Some of the world's most successful companies lost their competitive edge because they expanded into too many products and services.

Wise people simplify their lives. They periodically and prayerfully evaluate whether they need to move on from something.

Do you have trouble saying no? Are you spread too thin? Do you feel like you don't have enough time or energy to focus on your primary gifts and calling? If so, I highly recommend a book by Dr. Henry Townsend, Necessary Endings. In his book, Dr. Townsend compares the activities of life to a rosebush. He says that rosebushes produce more buds than the plant can sustain.

> "In order for the bush to thrive, a certain number of buds must go," writes Townsend. "The caretaker constantly examines the bush to see which buds are worthy of the plant's limited fuel and support and cuts the others away. He prunes them. Takes them away, never to return. In doing so, the gardener frees those needed resources so the plant can redirect them to the buds with the greatest potential to become mature roses."[78]

Think about that for a moment. Are you investing your time, energy, and resources in those things with the potential for the greatest return? The things that you are uniquely called and gifted to do?

Or are you spreading your resources into so many activities that you have very little time for the things you do best? If you want to reach your dreams, you will need to learn to say *no*.

What needs to end in your life to create space and resources for something new?

To answer this question, start by evaluating how you spend your time. Write down a list of all the work or ministry-related tasks you do over a three-to-four-week period, and how much time you spend on each. Categorize each task. Examples of categories may include meetings, writing, speaking, planning, coaching, book-keeping, marketing, miscellaneous paperwork, phone calls, presentations, administration, web design, responding to emails, etc. Obviously, the categories will be unique to your occupation. After sorting your tasks into categories, write down how much time you spent on each.

Then, ask yourself, *How much of my time was spent on the categories that reflect my primary gifts, calling, and core values? How much time was spent on everything else?*

Then get out the shears and start chopping. Be ruthless. Cut away or delegate every unnecessary activity that is standing in the way of pursuing your passions and purpose.

If you're like most people, there are many good things you could be doing with your time. The question is, do they reflect the *best* use of your time? Many people fill their to-do lists with things they believe are urgent. But there is a big difference between the urgent and the important. Learn to distinguish between the two.

I once mentored a woman who asked for advice on how to focus better. I asked, "What time of the day do you have the greatest physical and mental energy?" She said, "mornings." Then I asked her how she spent each morning in the past week. Almost every morning, she spent a good hour or so chatting on the phone or on Zoom with friends in a part of the country where the time zone was two hours later than hers. Friendships are a core value for her, and I understand that. But I advised her to tell her friends that she would love to connect, but that it needed to happen later in the day.

"You have to decide what your highest priorities are and have the courage—pleasantly, smilingly, non-apologetically, to say 'no' to other things," says Steven Covey, author of *Seven Habits of Highly Effective People.* "And the way you do that is by having a bigger 'yes' burning inside. The enemy of the "best" is often the "good."

Leadership guru John Maxwell said something similar. "If you focus your activities on the top 20 percent in terms of importance, you will have an 80 percent return on your investment. Successful leaders live according to the Law of Priorities. They recognize that activity is not necessarily accomplishment."

After you identify what you need to say "no" to, the next step is to write a plan with specific goals.

Set SMART Goals

Now that you have defined what activities need to end, it's time to set goals that line up with your mission.

You may have heard the term *SMART goals*. SMART is an acronym that represents a framework for setting effective goals. S – specific, M – measurable, A – achievable, R – realistic, T – time-bound. (SMART criteria are commonly attributed to Peter Drucker's concept of management.

S – Specific & Measurable: Studies show that only 15 percent of people define their goals in specific, measurable detail. A goal is a target, not a vague generalization.

If you haven't defined a specific destination, how will you know when you get there? And how will you measure your progress?

For example, let's say you want to lose ten pounds in six months and improve your general health. This is a commendable ambition, but it is not a goal. It is too general. And there is no way to measure it. How will you know when you have achieved it?

You could translate that desire into specific goals, as follows:

Goal 1: Eliminate junk food and cut back on unhealthy fats, starches, and sugars.

Goal 2: Improve general health and enhance weight loss by exercising aerobically four times a week for thirty-five minutes.

Goal 3: Reduce calories gradually, preferably with the advice of a doctor, naturopath, or nutritionist.

Goal 4: Meet in person or by phone or video chat with an accountability partner once every two weeks.

These goals provide tangible, practical, specific actions that will help you lose weight and improve your health.

Let's look at another example of how a vision can be translated into tangible goals. Perhaps you have a dream to build a successful Internet marketing business. You realize this will take time, and so you will continue working at your full-time job until your new business can support you and your family. What specific and measurable goals could you set to translate that dream into reality?

- One-week goal: Sign up for Internet marketing newsletters.
- One-month goals: Read two recently published

books on Internet marketing, subscribe to six Internet marketing e-newsletters, and watch two webinars or YouTube presentations conducted by respected internet marketing experts.

- Monthly goal starting in the second month: Read one book each month and continue online research.
- Three-month goal: Have met in person or online with three individuals with expertise in Internet marketing for advice and input.
- Fourth-month goal: Sign up for online coaching by a marketing expert.
- Six-month goal: Start a business plan, with the help of a coach or online tools. Continue the learning process.
- Nine-month goal: Complete business plan.
- Twelve-month goal: Launch website and start selling products.
- Two-year goal: Evaluate the financial feasibility of leaving daytime employment or cutting back hours to provide more time to focus on your business.

Obviously, you will need more action items than what I listed above, but these examples help illustrate the process for translating vision into specific, measurable goals. These are also achievable goals, which is the next criteria for SMART goals.

A – Achievable: Is your goal achievable? Dream big and aim high but stay grounded in reality. Be realistic about the amount of time you have to devote to your goals.

For example, if your goal is to be fully self-employed

in one month, but you haven't even started your new business, let alone developed it to where it is producing revenue, your goal is clearly not achievable.

Also, take into consideration the time necessary to acquire skills and experience. If you have never worked in the financial arena but have set a goal to obtain a position as vice-president of finance for a major corporation within one year, clearly your timing needs adjusting. The skills and expertise required to go from where you are to where you want to be are not achievable in such a short time frame.

Be careful to avoid the common trap of overestimating your efficiency. That inevitably leads to frustration. I know what that's like. For many years I scheduled more activities than I could possibly accomplish. After a brain injury from a car accident, I had several sessions with a brain injury specialist who helped me with scheduling and pacing. This involved placing limits on mental activities and scheduling frequent mental rests. For a task-oriented person like me, this was a difficult habit to develop. But it did help me to be more effective with scheduling and time management.

Realistic: Your goals should reflect the raw material God has placed in you. If you can't carry a tune, there's little point in setting a goal to become an internationally renowned soloist.

Also, you must evaluate whether you have the necessary skills to accomplish a goal. If not, how will you obtain those skills? Are you willing to invest the time and energy to develop new skills and competencies?

You must also ask yourself this crucial question: *Am I*

willing and able to make whatever sacrifices are necessary to work toward my goal? For example, if you would like to become part of a worship band, and you play piano at a basic level, are you willing to schedule sufficient practice time to develop the necessary competency?

If the answer is no, your goal is unrealistic.

Realistic does not imply easy. That's why *realistic* must never be used as an excuse for setting goals you can achieve with little work or sacrifice, or without divine intervention. Some people interpret realistic to mean *play it safe, stay within your limitations, don't push yourself.*

For a Christian, that is the opposite of living by faith. After all, if your dream isn't so big that you need God's grace and power to achieve it, then it's too small. Plus, big goals are more motivating than small ones. Small goals fail to ignite your passion.

T – Time-bound: Goals need a sense of urgency. Otherwise it's too easy to procrastinate. With no deadline, there is no internal pressure to accomplish the goal.

Use a Planner

Today, many, if not most people use digital calendars like Apple Calendar, Outlook, or Google Calendar. Outlook is my primary planner for detailed planning. But I use Apple Calendar for out of office meetings and appointments. Digital calendars allow you to sync your schedule across your devices, as well as set up calendars that include family members or co-workers.

However, many people prefer the old-fashioned method of using paper and pen or a printed planner. It doesn't matter what method you use. What matters is that you choose a method that works for you.

Schedule at least a half hour each week to plan. Start by reviewing the previous week. How did you do? What were your successes and failures? Did you stay focused and accomplish your scheduled tasks? If not, why not? Did you set too many goals by overestimating how much you can accomplish in a day?

This exercise will hold you accountable for how you spend your time.

Next, list your primary goals for the upcoming week. Evaluate the important versus the urgent. Prioritize your tasks with some type of ranking system. For example, you could use A for your highest priority items, B for those that are important but not urgent, and C for activities that are not essential and could be left undone that week if necessary.

Do you have faith for your dream?

Finally, in addition to these practical principles for goal setting, it is important to measure your goal in light of your faith.

Do you truly have faith for your dream? I'm not talking about pie-in-the-sky desires or hopeful fantasies or selfish ambitions. I'm referring to that deep, abiding faith that grows the more you pray about it and the more you take steps toward it. This is the kind of faith that will sustain you during those inevitable seasons of life when you face opposition and discouragement.

Dreams remain abstract until they are translated into steps. Developing an action plan is the bridge between what you believe and what you will achieve. An action plan doesn't mean boxing God into your schedule. It means creating a framework that allows your faith to be expressed through action.

Plans bring focus, accountability, and momentum. They help you say "no" to distractions so you can say a louder "yes" to God's purpose.

God does not despise structure; He often works through it. So start small, start specific, and start with faith. A written plan may look ordinary on paper, but when combined with a God-given dream and enduring faith, it becomes a powerful tool to change your life, and even more important, the lives of many others.

PART IV – FULFILL YOUR MISSION

OVERCOME OBSTACLES, TRIUMPH THROUGH TESTS, USE WHAT YOU HAVE

And we desire that each one of you show the same diligence to the full assurance of hope until the end, that you do not become sluggish, but imitate those who through faith and patience inherit the promises.[79]

CHAPTER TWELVE
OVERCOME OBSTACLES

If you saw the first Star Wars movie, you'll remember that a cruel emperor named Darth Vader had taken over the galaxy and evil had spread through the entire empire. Vader's dark forces had also taken captive the beautiful Princess Leia in an effort to stop the rebellion against the evil empire. But a brave young farmer named Luke Skywalker saved the day. Together with Obi-Wan Kenobi and two lovable droids, he rescued the princess, led an attack against the world-destroying battle station, and restored freedom and justice to the galaxy.

For more than forty-five years, the various Star Wars movies have entertained generations and remained one of the most successful franchises of all time.

At the time of writing, the most recent movie (*The Rise of Skywalker*), had grossed over $1 billion. The 2015 movie *The Force Awakens* has been the most successful to date, grossing over $2.5 billion and becoming just the third movie of all time to pass the $2 billion milestone. In total the combined box office revenues of the films have surpassed $10 billion. When you add other income like TV and merchandise sales, the total revenue has surpassed $46 billion.

What is the secret to the enduring success of Star Wars? The prevailing theory is that most people, regardless of age or background, are attracted to stories about the epic battle between good and evil, justice and injustice, and heroes versus villains. In each movie, fans sit on the edge of their seats waiting to see if the heroes will give up, run away, and let darkness spread over the innocent. Or will they risk their lives to stand up and bravely fight evil against overwhelming odds?

We all want to see the good guy or gal win. We all want to see good overcome evil. We love heroes like Luke Skywalker in *Star Wars*, Simba in *The Lion King*, or young Gerda in the *Snow Queen*. It's why we love stories like *The Little Engine that could*, *Finding Nemo*, and *Hansel and Gretel*. It's also why the crime show *NCIS* was the most watched drama series in the world over the past decade, hitting 1000 episodes in 2024, and reaching a cross-platform audience of more than 300 million people. *Law and Order* and the various FBI shows (*FBI, FBI Most Wanted,* and *FBI International*) followed close behind.

We all want to see heroes and heroines stand up to wicked witches, evil kings, cruel dictators, and dark empires, and against all odds prevail over injustice and save the innocent.

And whether we realize or not, there is something inside of most of us that longs to be the hero or heroine of our own story and the stories of those we love.

The Battle of Faith

As followers of Christ, we are fighting far more serious villains than wicked witches and evil kings. We are fighting against both internal and external villains that try to keep us from fulfilling our divine purpose. And overcoming these villains is vital if we are to be effective in fulfilling our purpose and expanding the kingdom.

The villains we face are primarily spiritual, working through circumstances, people, spiritual forces of darkness, and our own beliefs and attitudes. Whatever form they take, God has called us to overcome.

Dictionary definitions of the term *overcome* include:

- To get the better of in a struggle or conflict; conquer; defeat: to overcome the enemy.
- to prevail over (opposition, a debility, temptations, etc.); surmount: to overcome one's weaknesses.
- To defeat, overpower, prevail over (an enemy, a person, or thing opposing one, etc.).

Most of those definitions are military terms.

Did you know that the Bible also uses numerous military terms? In fact, the Bible's second most frequently used metaphor to describe a Christian is *soldier*, and the most frequently used metaphor to describe our journey of faith is *battle*.

From Genesis to Revelation, you'll find hundreds of military terms like fight, conquer, battle, strive, war, contend, guard, overcome, adversary, enemy, weapons, armor, soldier, and victory.

God has called us to overcome. The good news is that we don't have to do that on our own. Nor can we. He has provided all we need to fight and win the good fight of faith.

As a Canadian, I'm aware that we have a reputation around the world as peacemakers who are polite, passive, non-confrontational, and non-assertive.

But when it comes to winning the battles of life, being polite, passive, and non-confrontational is not an option. Avoiding battle is not an option. Sitting back and doing nothing while we experience one defeat after another is not an option. Not if you want to become the man or woman that God created you to be, not if you want to have the best possible marriage and family, not if you want to succeed in life, and not if you want to fulfill your destiny and purpose.

The Bible calls it, the good fight of faith.[80] Near the end of his life, the apostle Paul said, "I have fought the good fight, I have finished the race, I have kept the faith." [81]

You may as well accept from the get-go that your personal pathway of purpose is laden with obstacles and opposition. The bigger your dream, and the greater potential for that dream to glorify God and expand His kingdom – the more roadblocks, disappointments, and frustrations you will encounter along the way.

When you step out in faith, the enemy will do everything he can to try and discourage you, throw obstacles in your way, and besiege you with doubt. He will drop thoughts in your mind about all the reasons why you are inadequate. Why? He wants to scare you away from your God-ordained destiny.

Remember when God said that the Promised Land (Canaan) would be prolific with milk and honey, flowing rivers, lush gardens, sweet fruit, abundant grain, and choice wines? Sometimes we forget that it was also characterized by some less-desirable things – like menacing nine-foot giants, walled cities, hostile armies, and a host of other enemies that would fight and oppose the Israelites each step of the way.

How badly do you want your dream? How much are you willing to sacrifice to step into God's destiny for your life? The pathway of purpose is not an easy path. It takes determination, tenacity, courage, character, and faith. It requires patience, for it will take much longer than you had expected. It will be uncomfortable and sometimes painful. It will require tenacious faith, daily dependence on Jesus, and the willingness to confront your doubts, fears, and insecurities.

Are you willing to press through the obstacles, fears, and lies of the enemy to step into your destiny? If so, get ready to face one obstacle after another on the path to your dream.

For the remainder of this chapter, we will look at five of the most common obstacles we must all face and overcome.

1. Fear

I've heard it said, "Feeling afraid is sin. It means you don't have faith." That is not biblical. *Feelings* of fear are not sin – it's what you do with those feelings that matter. It is not wrong to *feel* fear. It is wrong to let fear dictate your actions, or lack of actions.

Are you committed to fulfilling the call of God on your life? If so, the question is not, "Will you encounter fear?" You will. The question is, "What will you do with the fear?"

It was Franklin Roosevelt who first said, "Courage is not the absence of fear; rather, it is the assessment that something else is far more important than my fear."

The Bible exhorts us to be courageous. But the fact is, you can't be courageous without fear.

Do you believe your calling is more important than your feelings of fear? Is it more important than your emotions? You don't need courage to do something that you are comfortable doing. You do need courage to do the things you fear. And because God has called us to live by faith, He will always lead us to do things that intimidate us. Why? He wants to strengthen our faith and deepen our trust in Him.

The first step to overcoming fear is to be honest with yourself about *why* you fear.

People avoiding the risk of failure might tell themselves that they are being practical and responsible, making sure all their ducks are in a row before taking a step of faith. Others might tell themselves: *It's just not God's timing. When it's God's timing I won't feel all this fear and trepidation.* Those who cling to comfort and security might tell themselves: *That's just not me – I could never do something like that.* Those who fear criticism and care more about people's opinions of them than they do about

God's, might use the excuse: *It's not loving to share my beliefs about controversial issues. We just need to be nice to everybody.*

Start by asking yourself, *What is the root of my fear?* Sometimes, we fear because we are not secure in God's unconditional love. If that's you, I encourage you research scriptures about the love and faithfulness of God and meditate on them regularly until you gain a deep heart revelation about God's character. Here's one example:

> *...that Christ may dwell in your hearts through faith; that you, being rooted and grounded in love, may be able to comprehend with all the saints what is the width and length and depth and height— to know the love of Christ which passes knowledge; that you may be filled with all the fullness of God.*[82]

In this chapter, I want to focus on what I believe to be the most important key to overcoming fear: choosing to act in obedience to God regardless of obstacles or feelings of fear. In other words, feel fear, but do it anyways.

Remember David? Little 17-year-old David was the son that Dad would not allow to fight in the army because he was the smallest and weakest of all his sons. So, David was given the job of looking after sheep, while all his brothers served in the much more prestigious role as soldiers in the Israeli army.

One day Dad asked David to take provisions to his brothers who were fighting with the Israeli army– all of whom were big, strong, muscular, soldiers. David gathered provisions and headed out to the army camp to seek his brothers.

As he approached the camp, he couldn't believe what

he was seeing. A giant Philistine by the name of Goliath was taunting and mocking the armies of Israel, challenging any one among them to meet him in one-on-one combat.

"Choose a man for yourselves, and let him come down to me," the giant taunted. "I defy the armies of Israel this day; give me a man, that we may fight together."[83]

Terrified, not one Israeli soldier responded. And it's no wonder: Goliath was just under ten feet tall; his armor weighed 126 pounds and the head on his iron spear weighed sixteen pounds.

When David saw that the Israeli soldiers were paralyzed with fear, too intimidated to stand up to Goliath, he was astonished. Remember, at the time, David was a simple shepherd's boy. He had not been trained in warfare like his brothers and the other Israeli soldiers. He had no armor or weapons or military skills.

But because of His zeal for God, he stood up and said, "Who is this uncircumcised Philistine that he should defy the armies of the living God?"[84]

When David's brothers mocked him, I love how David responded: "Is there not a cause?"[85] In other words, Is there not a purpose more important than fear?

When David said he would go and fight Goliath, King Saul discouraged him. "You are not able to go against this Philistine to fight with him; for you are a youth, and he a man of war from his youth." But David disagreed. "The Lord, who delivered me from the paw of the lion and from the paw of the bear, He will deliver me from the hand of this Philistine."[86]

As he stepped out to face Goliath, David refused King Saul's offer of weapons and armor and instead went to a stream and chose five smooth stones. He already had a sling with him – that's because Israeli shepherds used slings and stones to protect their flocks from predators. The sling was an everyday tool he used to protect his sheep.

> *"You come to me with a sword, with a spear, and with a javelin," David said to Goliath. "But I come to you in the name of the Lord of hosts, the God of the armies of Israel, whom you have defied. This day the Lord will deliver you into my hand, and I will strike you and take your head from you... Then all this assembly shall know that the Lord does not save with sword and spear; for the battle is the Lord's, and He will give you into our hands.* [87]

You know the end of the story. David was aware of his human weakness and insufficiency. He knew that in himself, he was utterly defenceless against Goliath. But he acted in courage, trusting that God would deliver him. And through the power of God, he defeated the mighty Goliath and saved the Israeli army.

What about you? Is your calling and purpose not more important than feelings of fear and intimidation? Are the people God wants you to minister to not more valuable than your feelings?

Courage is feeling fear but doing it anyways. Courage is not an emotion; it's an action.

James wrote, "So too, faith, if it does not have works [to back it up], is by itself dead [inoperative and ineffective]."[88]

We must put feet to our faith. Without a corresponding

action, faith is powerless. True heart faith is expressed with acts of obedience, which then activates the power of God. God's power and provision follow our steps of obedience.

James points to Abraham as an example of this.

Was not Abraham our father justified by works when he offered Isaac his son on the altar? Do you see that faith was working together with his works, and by works his faith was made perfect.[89]

Human nature says, "Lord I'm waiting for you to move. After you set me free from my fears, then I will step out." But if you are waiting until all the anxious feelings are gone before you step out in faith, you will wait forever.

Run from your fears and eventually they will rule you. They will enslave you. Each time you surrender to fear, it gains another foothold in your soul and life. The longer you wait to deal with it, the more areas of your life it will invade.

There is only one way to face fear—head on. When you confront your fears, you will be amazed by the confidence, liberty, and strength that result. Each time you conquer one fear, you become stronger, and new doors of opportunity will open to you. Every step moves you closer to the person God created you to be, releasing you into greater measures of your purpose.

To some degree, fear will always be with us. Why? Every time we step out in faith to obey God, despite feelings of intimidation, we grow. Our faith grows. Our character grows. As a result, God opens new opportunities because He can trust us with greater responsibilities. With each new venture, we must cross a new threshold of intimidation. Thus to some degree, *feelings* of fear will always be the price of living with purpose.

What fear is God asking you to face? What mountain of intimidation stands between you and your calling?

When you face your fears in God's strength, you will experience His awesome power working on your behalf. Not only will His grace carry you; it will lift you above the mountains of intimidation to experience wonderful new horizons of purpose. You will be set free to become the person you were created to be, liberated to embrace the wonderful destiny that God has for your life!

2. Doubt and Unbelief

Have you ever heard of the term *spatial disorientation*? It's not everyday term; it is an aviation term that I learned from my husband Brian's stories about airplane crashes that occurred during his first career as an air traffic controller.

Spatial disorientation was the cause of the helicopter crash in 2020 that killed MBA star Kobe Bryant, his daughter, the pilot, and several passengers.

What is spatial disorientation? It is when a pilot is not able to correctly interpret aircraft altitude, direction, or airspeed in relation to the earth or obstacles like trees, mountains, poles, or buildings. In the Bryant crash, the weather and visibility were extremely poor, and the pilot lost his bearings to the extent that he told air traffic control he was climbing in altitude, when he was actually descending.

Spatial disorientation is one of the most common

reasons for plane crashes involving small airplanes and helicopters. It typically happens at night or in poor weather, when there is low or no visibility, and the pilot cannot see the horizon. When the pilot can't rely on vision, other senses kick in. The problem is, when you are n flight, the variations in gravity, speed, and motion severely distort those senses; they alter the brain's perception of orientation and relative movement.

And that can be a disaster.

Pilots are trained to rely on their instrumentation panel, and not their senses, in poor visibility. But many pilots have said that when they can't see the horizon, the messages and feelings coming from their physical senses are so powerful that it takes an incredible amount of discipline to believe their instruments.

Just as a pilot can experience spatial disorientation in storms and poor visibility, many of God's beloved children experience spiritual disorientation when facing dark and stormy seasons in life. When we are trying to navigate in the night and we can't see what lies ahead, we may be tempted to rely on what our feelings or the circumstances or the evening news are telling us. Then the enemy, whom Jesus called the father of lies, takes advantage of our moments of weakness by dropping negative and depressing thoughts in our minds.

What is the solution? We must learn to get to know and rely on the spiritual instruments God has given us.

Our Spiritual Instrumentation Panel

At all times, and especially during dark seasons of the soul, it is vital that we focus on our spiritual instrumentation panel, which is the word of God. We need to learn to trust those instruments, no matter what is going on around us.

When a pilot can't see the horizon and must make a split-second decision, he won't have time to search through the aircraft manual on the flight deck. He needs to be intimately acquainted with the manual as well as the instrumentation panel. And he needs to have complete trust that those instruments provide accurate readings, regardless of the messages coming from his senses.

It's the same with us. It is not enough to have a dozen Bibles in different translations, or all the latest Bible apps on our phones and tablets. That will do us no good whatsoever unless we get that word IN us. We need spiritual revelation in our hearts, not merely superficial mental knowledge. Apart from the word of God, our faith has no foundation. All it takes is a little bitty storm to knock us down.

Are you flying by the instruments? When the storms of adversity surround you and pummel your finances, health, occupation, family, or ministry, what do you do? Do you succumb to doubt and place your trust in circumstances, your feelings, or the negative messages of our culture? Or do you place your trust in the word of God?

The Bible is not mere words on a page. The scriptures have supernatural power to move mountains of doubt.

"The word that God speaks is alive and full of power," says the writer of Hebrews, "making it active, operative, energizing, and effective." [90]

The psalmist wrote, "Forever, O Lord, Your word

is settled in heaven. Your faithfulness endures to all generations." [91]

God will always honour His word. He wants us to be so deeply rooted in His word, that no matter what is going on around us, we trust in His word more than our feelings or circumstances.

In the gospel of Matthew, Jesus talked about two groups of people: those who build their lives on the word of God, and those who don't.

> *"Therefore whoever hears these sayings of Mine, and does them, I will liken him to a wise man who built his house on the rock: and the rain descended, the floods came, and the winds blew and beat on that house; and it did not fall, for it was founded on the rock.*
>
> *"But everyone who hears these sayings of Mine, and does not do them, will be like a foolish man who built his house on the sand: and the rain descended, the floods came, and the winds blew and beat on that house; and it fell. And great was its fall."*[92]

It's not enough to know what the Bible says, we need to live what it says. We need to build every area of our lives on the word of God. That's the only way that we can remain standing in faith when we are besieged by doubts.

Remember when God gave Joshua instructions to prepare him to lead the Israelites into the land of promise?

> *This Book of the Law shall not depart from your mouth, but you shall meditate in it day and night, that you may observe to do according to all that is written in it. For then you will make your way prosperous, and then you will have*

good success.[93]

This passage contains both a promise and a warning. To paraphrase, God said, "Son, if you want to succeed, if you want to receive the promises I have given you, if you want to prosper in this new place I am leading you to possess, there is a condition. You must continually meditate on My word. Then you must obey it."

When your journey takes you through a dark valley of the soul, doubts will overwhelm you. That's the time to refresh and remind yourself of God's promises to you. Read them, pray them, declare them, and thank God for them. As you do, faith will rise up in your heart and the doubts will dissipate.

Then stand. Refuse to be moved by the storms that surround you. God is faithful, and His word never fails.

3: Comparison

Comparing yourself to others will leave you feeling frustrated, inferior, and anxious. A recent study found that more than 75 percent of people reported feeling envious of someone in the last year.

Paul warned against comparing ourselves with others: "But they, measuring themselves by themselves, and comparing themselves among themselves, are not wise." [94]

Compare and you will despair. It's a losing game. *I'll never be as gifted a writer as Max Lucado or Beth Moore, so what's the point in trying?* Or, *I'll never be able to get a recording contract like Ben Fielding or Chris Tomlin or Jenn Johnson, so why should I work on my music career?*

There will always be someone more gifted, talented, or

qualified than you. There will always be someone who has achieved greater success in living a dream like yours.

God wants to engage every one of us in a vision that is far greater than our natural abilities or resources. But we must stop focusing on what we don't have compared to others.

> *Pay careful attention to your own work, for then you will get the satisfaction of a job well done, and you won't need to compare yourself to anyone else. For we are each responsible for our own conduct.*[95]

On several occasions, I have fallen into the trap of comparing myself with others who are more talented. As soon as I started comparing myself, I felt intimidated. I felt like I want to bury my gifts rather than risk rejection.

When this happens, I remind myself of the words of the Henry Van Dyke: "The woods would be silent if no birds sang except those that sang best."

You'll never be happy and productive if you keep comparing yourself with others. But you can experience joy in knowing that you are doing your best with what God has given you.

4: Perfectionism

In his book *Art & Fear*, author David Bayles tells the story of a ceramics teacher who divided his class into two groups. He said that the first group would be graded on the quantity of the work; the second group on the quality. He wrote:

> Grading time came and a curious fact emerged: the works of highest quality were all produced by the group being graded for quantity. It seems while the

"quantity" group was busily churning out piles of work and learning from their mistake, the "quality" group had sat theorizing about perfection, and in the end had little more to show for their efforts than grandiose theories and a pile of dead clay.[96]

Years ago, I thought that waiting on the Lord meant coming to a full stop until I had crystal clear discernment of the path forward. In time I realized that attitude was not only wrong; it was also based on the fear of failure and a lack of trust in God. Yes, we need to hear from the Lord. Yes, we need to wait on Him. But that does not mean we can expect Him to give us a detailed road map of not only what to do, but how to do it, and what to expect each step along the way.

Perfectionists may be motivated by a commitment to excellence, at least initially. Unfortunately, the line between excellence and perfectionism is blurry at best. I can think of times when I started a project with a desire for excellence, but at some point, slipped into perfectionism. Inevitably, I paid the price with stress, frustration, and delays in accomplishing my goals.

How do we know we have crossed the line from excellence into perfectionism? One way is to ask yourself the question, *Do I fear the consequences of not doing well? Is that fear with me when I am doing a task? Is it difficult for me to consider that a project is complete? Am I always trying to improve it?*

Sometimes, we don't want to step out in faith because we are afraid of looking foolish in the eyes of others if we fail. Perfectionists often have an unhealthy need for other people's approval. We might have thoughts like *If I try something new, will I look like a fool? What if I fail? What will people think? If I tell people my dreams, will they laugh at me?*

It's all too easy to become distracted by the opinions of others, wasting emotional energy worrying about what other people think about us.

One of the things that protects us from perfectionism is understanding the difference between fearing God, versus fearing man.

The fear of man brings a snare,
But whoever trusts in the Lord shall be safe.[97]

In the fear of the Lord there is strong confidence,
And His children will have a place of refuge.
The fear of the Lord is a fountain of life,
To turn one away from the snares of death.[98]

What is the fear of the Lord? It is a deep reverence and respect for God. The fear of the Lord creates a longing for holiness, and a desire to please and obey Him. It also protects us from what the Bible calls, "the fear of man". The fear of man is when we are more concerned about what other people think about us than we care about pleasing and obeying God.

Perfectionism wears many disguises. Some people are slaves to perfectionism but you would never know it, because their response is to simply take no risks and remain safe in their comfort zone.

Give yourself permission to fail. Learn to laugh at yourself when you make mistakes (while still learning from them). And most important, learn to receive God's forgiveness for failure and His grace to continue learning, growing, and developing a more Christ-like character.

5. Isolation

While it is that vital that we don't have an unhealthy need for approval from others, it is equally vital that we cultivate healthy relationships.

Isolation is the enemy of fulfillment and purpose. We all need friends to reach our dreams. The bigger your dream, the more opposition you are going to encounter. The greater barriers of fear, intimidation, and criticism you will need to push through. And you can't do that all on your own, no matter how strong your faith may be.

Pastor Chris Hodges said, "A dream is a compelling vision you see in your heart that's too big to accomplish without the help of others."

Some people want to do everything alone because they fear rejection by others. Others think they can get more done without having to deal with people. Whatever the reasons, you need friends to help you reach your dream. All of life is more meaningful when we prioritize connection.

Before Jesus fully launched His ministry, He built a team.

It's no coincidence that the Bible uses the phrase "body of Christ" to describe the community of believers. The imagery here is obvious, and yet, so many Christians, including Christian leaders, think they can fulfill their purpose outside of close relationships with other believers.

God designed us in such a way that it is not possible for one person or one ministry to accurately express the character and purposes of God. We can only fully express

God's character, love, giftings, and purpose when we function together in loving community.

The New Testament is packed with statements with the words "one-another." Love one another. Forgive one another. Edify one another. Spur one another on to love and good deeds. Accept one another. Pray for one another. Encourage one another.

The more we can engage in on-going deepening relationships, the more we experience the benefits: love, acceptance, edification, encouragement, transformation, exhortation, and challenge.

We all go through times of discouragement, disappointment, and self-doubt. Times when we have forgotten our dream or vision. A friend is someone who will remind us, and who will encourage us in our faith and in pursuing our dreams.

We need each other to fulfill the purpose and dreams that God has placed in our hearts.

6: Distractions

You may not consider distractions to be a major obstacle, but in our modern society, distractions may be the most sinister enemy of all. Why? Because most of us don't realize how much time and energy we waste on unimportant things.

Never before in human history have there been as many distractions as in western culture today. Technology was supposed to give us more time to focus on what's important; instead, it has become a huge distraction. Material wealth was supposed to give us more time. It has done the opposite, because of the amount of time people spend thinking about, shopping for, and maintaining their homes and possessions.

To stay focused, we must each periodically ask ourselves: *Is there anything that is taking up too much of my time, energy, and focus?* It might be social media for one person, shopping for another, entertainment for another. None of these things are bad in themselves. That's not the point. The point is, has overindulgence or imbalance distracted you from your calling?

Long distance runners know that to succeed, they must focus on the finish line. Nothing will throw a runner off stride or slow her down more than turning to look at the runner coming behind her or continually glancing at the crowds to see how they are reacting to her performance.

> *Therefore we also, since we are surrounded by so great a cloud of witnesses, let us lay aside every weight, and the sin which so easily ensnares us, and let us run with endurance the race that is set before us, looking unto Jesus, the author and finisher of our faith..."*[99]

Your race is your personal pathway of purpose, your calling, God's highest destiny for your life.

This verse of scripture warns of two major hindrances in winning the race: sin, and weights. Sin is easy enough to recognize, and we know what to do: repent. Weights are not so obvious. The NLT translation says, "let us strip off every weight that slows us down."

Long-distance runners know that extra pounds, whether in body weight or clothing, impede speed and performance. Weights represent anything that distracts you from focusing on your pathway of purpose. Those distractions will throw you off stride and sometimes steer you in a direction that leads you further from, rather than closer to, your dream.

Distractions come in many forms, such as obsessiveness with all our technical gadgets, social media, and material possessions.

But perhaps the distractions that hinder us most are those that come from our minds and hearts. Obsessing over minor annoyances and nuisances will distract you from the big picture. Keep your heart free of emotional clutter, your mind focused on positive thoughts, and your spirit continually attuned to God.

It all comes down to a choice between the good and the best, the mediocre and the excellent, the mundane and the significant.

Choose well, and at the end of your life, you will be able to say the same words as Paul: "I have fought the good fight, I have finished the race, I have kept the faith."[100]

Obstacles are not the end of the road—they are the proving ground of our faith, resilience, and purpose. Each obstacle is an opportunity to depend more fully on God's grace and strength to persevere.

Every challenge we overcome becomes a stepping stone toward the person we were created to be. The struggle refines us, the resistance strengthens us, and the journey reveals the beauty of perseverance.

In this you rejoice, though now for a little while, if necessary, you have been grieved by various trials, so that the tested genuineness of your faith—more precious than gold that perishes though it is tested by fire—may be found to result in praise and glory and honor at the revelation of Jesus Christ.[101]

CHAPTER THIRTEEN
TRIUMPH THROUGH TESTS

You've likely heard of the Navy Seals (SEALS), the U.S. Navy's primary special operations force. Although their operations are highly classified, the SEAL's public profile was raised by the extensive media coverage of Seal Team 6 killing terrorist Osama Bin Laden in 2011.

SEALS are proficient in unconventional warfare, special reconnaissance, demolition, and intelligence gathering in diverse and challenging environments.

Anyone who thinks they want to become a Navy Seal has to pass numerous physical and mental tests before they are even accepted into the training program. Once candidates are admitted into the program, they must then spend eighteen months of training that is so rigorous that about 80 percent don't make it.

Roughly three weeks into training, SEALS go through what the Navy calls "Hell Week." This involves 5½ days of cold, wet, brutally difficult operational training on fewer than four hours of sleep. *Hell Week* tests physical endurance, mental toughness, psychological stability, pain and cold tolerance, sleep deprivation, teamwork, attitude, and a person's ability to perform work under extreme physical and mental stress. On average, only 25 percent of SEAL candidates make it through *Hell Week*, the toughest training in the U.S. Military.[102]

Why must they undergo such arduous tests and training? SEALS must develop resilience, physical and mental toughness, and the ability to quickly adapt to unexpected situations to prepare them to deal with hundreds of potential challenges that could keep them from succeeding at any given mission. And even with all that preparation and training, most SEAL teams still encounter numerous unexpected obstacles, that require instant decisions and reactions.

When it comes to developing spiritual resilience and maturity, we also undergo a lifelong series of trials and tests to help transform our character and prepare us for greater effectiveness in serving God and expanding His kingdom.

"Adversity is not simply a tool," wrote Charles Stanley. "It is God's most effective tool for the advancement of our spiritual lives."

> *Consider it wholly joyful, my brethren, whenever you are enveloped in or encounter trials of any sort or fall into various temptations. Be assured and understand that*

the trial and proving of your faith bring out endurance and steadfastness and patience. But let endurance and steadfastness and patience have full play and do a thorough work, so that you may be [people] perfectly and fully developed [with no defects], lacking in nothing.[103]

Trials and Tests Prepare you for Your Destiny

As I'm sure you have already discovered, we face many trials on our journey of faith – trials designed to grow us and mould us more into the image of Christ. God's loving purpose through the tests and trials is to mature our faith and character so that we can responsibly steward increasing measures of responsibility and influence for His glory.

The trials and tests God allows in your life are a blessing, not a curse. They are stepping stones to fulfilling your dreams. Without maturity of character, the influence God wants to entrust to you can destroy you, others around you, and the reputation of Christ's church.

You have likely heard the quote by Lord Acton, "Power tends to corrupt, and absolute power corrupts absolutely." Power can lead to pride, entitlement, or a belief that one is above the rules. Over time, small compromises can lead to major ethical failures. We have all seen what happens when powerful leaders lack a godly character.

God cares much more about our character than our comfort. And the greater the influence He wants to entrust to us, the more Christ-like character we need to handle it with integrity.

Words like *trials, refining,* and *tests* occur more than

two hundred times in scripture. These tests are never for God's benefit. After all, he's God. He already knows what is in our hearts. Tests are for our benefit, to reveal wrong, insincere, or divided motivations and attitudes, so that with God's help we can deal with them.

The refining pot is for silver and the furnace for gold,
But the Lord tests the hearts.[104]

Squeeze a sponge and the gunk on the inside oozes to the surface. Heart tests work much the same way; pressures in the form of difficult circumstances squeeze hidden soul toxins to the surface where we can see them.

It's easy to be a fountain of joy and peace when life is good. It's easy to be kind, loving, and generous when people are treating us well. But even unbelievers can do that. It's when we face pressure, pain, and persecution that we find out what's really in our hearts.

Adversity and suffering reveal the weak spots in my relationship with God. When someone wrongly accuses or betrays me, or hurts someone I love, I find out just how forgiving I am. When I'm late for a meeting and somebody cuts me off on the freeway, I find out how much patience and self-control I have. When I am sleep deprived, I find out how much joy and gentleness I have. When I experience a tragedy or setback, I find out how much I trust in God's goodness and sovereignty.

Many times, I've been disappointed by my reaction to pain and stress. But I'm also grateful when those flaws are revealed, because I desire to grow in godliness.

Sometimes negative circumstances are the result of Satanic opposition. Jesus said that Satan's purpose is to kill, steal, and destroy. He also said, "I give you the authority to trample on serpents and scorpions, and over all the power of the enemy.[105] We need spiritual discernment to recognize these attacks and address them, with the spiritual armor and weapons outlined in scripture (see Ephesians chapter six).

Some people blame the devil for everything, including their own sins and the consequences of those sins. Others believe that if you are living by faith, you should never experience difficulty or pain. Neither of those attitudes are biblical. Yes, we have a spiritual enemy and God has given us authority to address demonic attacks and oppression. But we also need to understand that there are many difficulties God allows in our lives to build our character and mature our faith.

Tests come in many forms. We must recognize these tests so that we can respond in a godly manner.

Joseph

If any Bible character exemplified facing and maturing through trials and tests, it was Joseph.

Joseph endured much affliction and pain, including betrayal, adversity, temptation, unanswered prayers, humiliation, false accusations, unjust punishment, and loneliness.

Why did Joseph suffer so much adversity? God tells us why:

God sent a man before them—
Joseph—who was sold as a slave.
They hurt his feet with fetters,
He was laid in irons.
Until the time that his word came to pass,

The word of the Lord tested him.[106]

The New Living translation of the last phrase reads: "Until the time came to fulfill his dreams, the Lord tested Joseph's character."

Through a thirteen-year journey of adversity, God grew Joseph into a man to whom He could entrust mind-boggling levels of resources, influence, and responsibility. Most important, Joseph's position enabled him to save his father and brothers from dying in a famine, thus preserving the Jewish race.

Many of Joseph's trials and tests are similar to what you and I also face in our journey of faith. Let's look at a few of those tests and how we can respond in a way that will strengthen our faith and mature our character.

The Test of Betrayal

Joseph's trials of faith began when he was only seventeen years old, when God gave him two dreams that he would be elevated to a place of great authority that surpassed that of his brothers and father.

Because of Joseph's birth order, those were very unusual dreams. He was the eleventh of twelve sons. In that culture, the eldest son was granted legal and spiritual birthright, inheritance, and family authority. As son number eleven, Joseph was a nobody in terms of his standing in the family and community. Yet he dreamt he would have authority over all his brothers, even his father.

When he told his father and brothers about his dreams, his brothers were deeply offended. They already hated Joseph because he was their father's favourite son.

And his brothers said to him, "Shall you indeed reign over us? Or shall you indeed have dominion over us?" So they hated him even more for his dreams and for his words.[107]

One day, Joseph was taking some food out to his brothers in the field. They saw him coming, and they said, "Look, this dreamer is coming! Come therefore, let us now kill him and cast him into some pit; and we shall say, 'Some wild beast has devoured him.' We shall see what will become of his dreams!"[108]

The eldest brother talked them out of murder and convinced them to instead sell Joseph as a slave to some Midianites who were passing by. Then the brothers lied and let their father believe that Joseph was killed by wild animals.

The Midianites who purchased Joseph took him to Egypt and sold him as a slave to Potiphar, who was one of Pharoah's officers.

Can you imagine what that was like for Joseph? To receive a wonderful dream from God and then everything that could go wrong, goes wrong? Maybe that has happened to you. If so, take heart. God is faithful, and in His time and in His way, He will fulfill your purpose.

Joseph's nightmare kept getting worse. Even though Joseph kept his heart pure by continuing to honour God and serve faithfully as a slave, one day, he was falsely accused of rape and thrown into a prison.

That's where he spent the next thirteen years of his life.

In the same way God used adversity to prepare Joseph for his ultimate purpose, God does the same with us.

The Test of Faithfulness

Faithfulness is of far greater value to God than our spiritual gifts or natural abilities. Lots of people have amazing gifts and big dreams. But if they do not develop a faithful character, those dreams will never go anywhere. Joseph's first test of faithfulness occurred during his time as a slave in Potiphar's house:

> *The Lord was with Joseph, and he was a successful man; and he was in the house of his master the Egyptian. And his master saw that the Lord was with him and that the Lord made all he did to prosper in his hand. So Joseph found favor in his sight, and served him. Then he made him overseer of his house, and all that he had he put under his authority. So it was, from the time that he had made him overseer of his house and all that he had, that the Lord blessed the Egyptian's house for Joseph's sake; and the blessing of the Lord was on all that he had in the house and in the field.*[109]

Joseph started out as one of many nameless slaves in Potiphar's house. But Joseph worked harder than all the other slaves. He honoured God by giving his best to his master, even though Potiphar was a heathen. As a result, God's favor was on him and Joseph was promoted to chief slave and assigned authority in the household.

What does the scripture mean when it says Joseph was *successful*? In western culture most people equate success with financial riches, fame, freedom, power, and fun. Does the fact that Joseph was successful mean that he got to lounge around drinking Starbucks lattes and giving orders to the other slaves while he impressed the servant girls with his iPad? Did Potiphar give Joseph an expense account, so he could buy Armani suits and take luxury vacations at five-star resorts on the Egyptian Nile?

Of course not. Make no mistake, Joseph was still a slave. He did not earn a wage. His time was not his own and he had to work hard from early morning until late at night. He had no freedom. He had none of the comforts we often associate with the terms *success* and *prosperity*.

Nonetheless, Joseph prospered. He prospered inwardly, in the grace and peace of God. And every project assigned to him prospered because God's favor was on him.

Joseph's heart attitude and commitment to excellence in working for a heathen master in unjust circumstances was the same as though he was serving God.

Now, that's faithfulness.

How did Potiphar reward Joseph for his faithful service? He threw him in prison after Potiphar's wife falsely accused him of rape.

But even in prison, Joseph once again served faithfully.

> *But the Lord was with Joseph and showed him mercy, and He gave him favor in the sight of the keeper of the prison. And the keeper of the prison committed to Joseph's hand all the prisoners who were in the prison; whatever they did there, it was his doing. The keeper of the prison did not look into anything that was under Joseph's authority, because the Lord was with him; and whatever he did, the Lord made it prosper.*[110]

Joseph had no idea *why* he had to suffer through slavery in a heathen household in a heathen nation, or later, why he spent so many years in a cold, rat-infested prison. But he did know God. He had an intimate relationship with God. Because of that he understood the importance of faithfulness.

Joseph spent thirteen years serving in circumstances that were the exact opposite of his dream. None of those circumstances represented what most of us would consider a "divine assignment." After all, what does slavery or prison have to do with preparing for the role of Prime Minister of Egypt, entrusted with mind-boggling levels of wealth, resources, and authority?

Everything! Each of those assignments were opportunities for Joseph to learn faithfulness in the small things so God could prepare him for greater things.

Jesus said: "He who is faithful in what is least is faithful also in much; and he who is unjust in what is least is also unjust in much....If you have not been faithful in what belongs to another man, who will give you what is your own?"[111]

How can we cultivate greater faithfulness?

One is to serve in every responsibility and task – be that in the workplace, at home with your family, in the community, in ministry– as though you are serving God himself.

Many of us pick and choose when we will be faithful. We are willing to be faithful in performing certain tasks if we think it will get us where we want to go.

> *Whatever you do, work at it with all your heart, as working for the Lord, not for men, since you know you will receive an inheritance from the Lord as a reward.*[112]

You will face the test of faithfulness, not once, not twice, but time and time again. By the grace of God, choose faithfulness day in and day out, and it will become a habit. Habits form character. And godly character brings great joy to the heart of God.

The Test of Moral Purity

As already mentioned, when Joseph was a slave in Potiphar's house, he served faithfully, day in and day out.

Apparently, Joseph was also a very attractive man; the Bible says he was "handsome in form and appearance." Potiphar's wife noticed. And she lusted after Joseph.

And it came to pass after these things that his master's wife cast longing eyes on Joseph, and she said, "Lie with me."

But he refused and said to his master's wife, "Look, my master does not know what is with me in the house, and he has committed all that he has to my hand. There is no one greater in this house than I, nor has he kept back anything from me but you, because you are his wife. How then can I do this great wickedness, and sin against God?"[113]

Potiphar's wife would not give up. Day after day she tried to seduce Joseph, but he kept saying "no". Finally, she became angry at Joseph's persistent rejection and went to her husband Potiphar and falsely accused Joseph of rape.

What happened? Potiphar believed his wife, became angry, and threw Joseph in prison.

Joseph's response to Potiphar's wife demonstrated his commitment to integrity and moral purity, regardless of the consequences. Many scriptures in the New Testament also speak of the importance of moral purity.

For this is the will of God, your sanctification: that you should abstain from sexual immorality; that each of you should know how to possess his own vessel in sanctification and honour, not in passion of lust. [114]

Temptations come in many forms, not just sexual. Will you, like Joseph, choose moral purity when facing the temptation to compromise and sin?

The Test of Compassion

If I had suffered through the type of circumstances Joseph faced, I'm not sure I would be very kind or caring about people around me. Joseph, however, kept a soft heart towards God and others around him. He demonstrated kindness and compassion in every situation. One example is seen in how he helped his fellow prisoners.

The king's butler and baker had been confined to the same prison as Joseph, and one night, they both had a vivid dream, which they did not understand. In the morning, Joseph noticed they were sad.

So he asked Pharaoh's officers who were with him in the custody of his lord's house, saying, "Why do you look so sad today?"

And they said to him, "We each have had a dream, and there is no interpreter of it."

So Joseph said to them, "Do not interpretations belong to God? Tell them to me, please."[115]

Joseph's compassion is seen in his sensitivity to notice his fellow prisoners were sad, followed by his offer to help.

After the two fellow prisoners shared their dreams, Joseph provided an interpretation. He had good news and bad news. The good news was that the butler would be released from prison in three days; the bad news was that the baker would be executed. Joseph also asked the butler to remember him after he was released by speaking to Pharoah about him. (However, the butler forgot about Joseph until two years later when Pharoah had a dream).

Every one of us will face the test of compassion, time and again throughout our lives. It's easy to show compassion to others when they are kind to us, and when we are feeling well or enjoying our life circumstances. The test is to show kindness and compassion to those who hurt us, and to reach out to serve even when we feel discouraged or are facing adverse circumstances.

Remember when Jesus said the second greatest commandment is to love our neighbor as ourselves? Immediately He was asked, "Who is my neighbor?"

Jesus responded by telling the parable of the good Samaritan. A Jewish traveller was beaten and left half dead alongside a road. A Jewish priest came by, followed by a Jewish Levite. Both ignored the man. Finally, a Samaritan came by and helped the injured man, despite the fact that Jews and Samaritans typically refused to have anything to do with each other. He cleaned and bandaged his wounds, even taking him to an inn and paying for his food, lodging, and care.

"So which of these three do you think was neighbor to him who fell among the thieves?" Jesus asked.

And he said, "He who showed mercy on him."

Then Jesus said to him, "Go and do likewise."[116]

Jesus made it clear that the *neighbor* represented in the

second commandment is not referring to our families or friends at church (although they are included of course). Rather, our neighbor represents people in need, including perfect strangers, that God wants us to minister to.

We all have busy lives, and it's so easy to ignore the needs of those around us. Like Joseph, let's be quick to notice those who are sad and seek to love them however God directs, whether that is with a word of encouragement, prayer, or assistance with practical needs.

The Test of Patience

Throughout scripture, faith and patience go hand in hand. The writer of Hebrews challenges us to "imitate those who through faith and patience inherit the promises."

If anyone exemplified faith and patience, it was Joseph. For thirteen years, he endured difficult and painful circumstances. Was he tempted by doubt? Was he tempted to feel insecure in God's love? Was he tempted to question whether or not the dreams he had as a young man came from God? The Bible doesn't tell us whether he wrestled with thoughts and feelings of doubt, fear, and impatience. But whatever temptations or tumultuous emotions that Joseph may have experienced, he remained steadfast in trusting God.

Integrity is essential in passing the test of faith and patience. It is easy to obey God when things are going well. But when you lose your job or business and the bills are piling up, what do you do? Do you stop giving to God's work? Do you cheat on your income tax? Do you commit fraud?

On the path to your dream, you will be tempted by impatience and frustration. At that point, you may try to make things happen on your own. You will be most vulnerable to this temptation when you have seen no breakthroughs after a lengthy period of believing for God's promise. You've prayed and prayed. You have done whatever God showed you to do. But months, years, and perhaps even decades have come and gone, and you are still not seeing a breakthrough.

Deep down, you may begin to feel like the obstacles are insurmountable. You might question God's love for you, and His willingness or ability to intervene in your circumstances. That's when you will be tempted to compromise and settle for what you can accomplish through human effort.

That is also exactly what happened to Abram and Sarai. Ten years after God first gave Abram the promise that he would be the father of many nations, there was still no child. By then, Abram was eighty-five years old, and Sarai was seventy-six, not to mention the fact she had been barren her entire life. Understandably, they were discouraged. They were afraid. And I have no doubt they felt impatient and frustrated.

So, they devised a plan, a plan that the Bible describes as "according to the flesh."[117] The plan was simple: Abram would sleep with Sarai's maid Hagar in the hopes of conceiving an heir. It worked! In their minds, the plan was a huge success when Hagar conceived and bore Abram a son, whom he named Ishmael.

But Ishmael was the son of the flesh, not the son of God's promise. He was the result of Abram and Sarai trying to "help God out" by settling for what they could accomplish through human effort.

In our lives, Ishmael represents the times that we settle for a reduced version of God's will and vision that we can achieve on our own. Or we compromise biblical principles to try and make things happen when it seems God is not answering our prayers.

It happens when a single person has been praying and waiting a long time for a godly spouse, but nothing is happening. She begins to fear that God isn't going to come through for her. So she marries someone who is not a Christian, or someone who claims to be a Christian but does not have a genuine faith.

It happens when a person believes God has directed him to start a business, but nothing seems to go right. He begins to cheat on his taxes, or stop tithing, or incur bad debts.

This also happens when people settle for a "shadow" occupation or ministry. Perhaps you believe God has called you to write. You write a manuscript and send it off to publishers and receive nothing but rejection letters. As a result, you give up and settle for a life-long career as a proofreader. Or you believe God has called you to pastor a church. You have done your part; you have gone to Bible college and studied hard to prepare yourself, but the only positions you have been offered are in church maintenance, or office administration. So you give up on your dream.

When Ishmael was thirteen years old and Abram ninety-nine, God appeared to Abram again to reaffirm the promise and say that Sarai would bear the promised child. He also changed Abram's name to Abraham, and Sarai's name to Sarah.

Well, it appears Abraham was still not fully convinced. Look how he responded:

> *Then Abraham fell on his face and laughed, and said in his heart, "Shall a child be born to a man who is one hundred years old? And shall Sarah, who is ninety years old, bear a child?" And Abraham said to God, "Oh, that Ishmael might live before You!"*[118]

As you can see, Abraham was still trying to convince God to let Ishmael be the promised son. But God replied, "No, Sarah your wife shall bear you a son, and you shall call his name Isaac; I will establish My covenant with him for an everlasting covenant, and with his descendants after him."[119]

Then God said that Sarah would bear a son in one year's time. And that's exactly what happened. One year later, when Abraham was one hundred years old and Sarah was ninety, she gave birth to the promised son, Isaac.

God has a specific timing and strategy for the fulfillment of His vision and promises in your life. When nothing seems to be happening, remember God's words to Abraham and Sarah: "Is anything too hard for the Lord?"[120]

At the appointed time, the promise will come.

Patience is crucial as we pursue our passions and dreams. To prepare us for each new level of purpose, God leads us on a journey of character development. Sometimes that journey may seem as though it is taking forever. Still, it is vital to avoid the temptation to short-circuit the work God wants to do in our hearts.

Be patient with the process.

The Test of Readiness

If today God opened a major door of opportunity for you, how would you respond?

When Joseph's big opportunity came, he was ready.

Pharoah, the king of Egypt, had a vivid dream; the dream troubled him. He knew it was significant, but he did not know what it meant. Pharoah called for all the magicians and wise men in the nation of Egypt to come to the palace and tell him the meaning of his dream. But no-one could interpret the dream.

Then the king's butler, who had been with Joseph in prison two years previously, remembered that Joseph had correctly interpreted his dream. Who could have known that the butler Joseph ministered to in prison was a divine connection, a man God would use to give Joseph an audience with Pharoah?

The butler told Pharoah about Joseph's ability to interpret dreams, and Pharoah sent for him. "They brought him quickly out of the dungeon; and he shaved, changed his clothing, and came to Pharoah."[121]

Notice this opportunity demanded instant obedience. Joseph didn't have the option of saying to Pharoah's assistants, "Okay I'm willing to meet Pharoah, but first I need three days to fast and pray to ensure I can interpret his dream." You don't say things like that to Pharoah, not unless you have a death wish.

Joseph had to be ready. And he was ready, because of his close relationship with God.

Pharoah said to Joseph, "I have had a dream, and there is no one who can interpret it. But I have heard it said of you that you can understand a dream, to interpret it."[122]

Joseph's response showed his humility and trust in God when he replied: "It is not in me; God will give Pharoah an answer of peace."[123]

Joseph's very survival depended on accurately interpreting Pharoah's dream. After all, Pharoah had a well-known reputation for chopping off the heads of anyone who displeased him. Failure was not an option. But Joseph had such an intimate relationship with his Lord that he was fully confident God would come through for him.

Immediately, Joseph provided the interpretation. To summarize, he said that Egypt would have seven years of plenty, followed by seven years of severe famine, the worst famine in Egypt's history. But Joseph didn't stop there, even though all Pharoah had asked was that he interpret the dream.

With boldness and confidence, Joseph immediately followed the interpretation by recommending a divinely inspired economic strategy.

> *"Now therefore, let Pharaoh select a discerning and wise man, and set him over the land of Egypt. Let Pharaoh do this, and let him appoint officers over the land, to collect one-fifth of the produce of the land of Egypt in the seven plentiful years. And let them gather all the food of those good years that are coming, and store up grain under the authority of Pharaoh, and let them keep food in the cities. Then that food shall be as a reserve for the land for the seven years of famine which shall be in the*

land of Egypt, that the land may not perish during the famine."[124]

Pharoah was amazed at Joseph's wisdom and said to his servants, "Can we find such a one as this, a man in whom is the Spirit of God?"

Look what Pharoah said to Joseph:

"Inasmuch as God has shown you all this, there is no one as discerning and wise as you. You shall be over my house, and all my people shall be ruled according to your word; only in regard to the throne will I be greater than you." And Pharaoh said to Joseph, "See, I have set you over all the land of Egypt."[125]

Wow! After thirteen long years as a slave and prisoner, in just one day Joseph was elevated to the highest position in Egypt, second only to Pharoah.

Joseph had to be ready. And he was ready because of his devotion to God and his choice to act with faithfulness, honour, and integrity no matter what circumstances he faced. Through all the years of adversity, Joseph's character and faith had matured to the point that God could entrust Joseph with mind-boggling levels of influence, authority, and responsibility.

Are you ready to embrace divine opportunities? Do you have such a close relationship with God that you able to discern and respond when God opens a door of greater influence for His purposes?

The Test of Forgiveness

Perhaps the most difficult test we all face in our journey of faith is the test of forgiveness. And this is a test we will face time and time again.

As we have already seen, Joseph was mistreated, misunderstood, betrayed, abused, falsely accused, and rejected– not once, but time and time again. If anybody would be justified in becoming hard, resentful, and bitter, it was Joseph.

But he kept his heart right. How do we know that? By the way he responded to the things that happened to him.

It's one thing for your own family to betray you and sell you into slavery. That's bad enough. But to be falsely accused of rape? And thrown into a dark, cold, lonely prison? I think if I were Joseph, I would have really had it out with God. I likely would have thought, *What's with this God? I love you and serve you with all my heart, and this is what I get for it?*

Have you ever felt that way? You are doing your best to love and serve God, and calamity or sickness strikes you, or your business fails, or you lose a loved one. Does it feel like God has let you down?

For Joseph, the ultimate test of forgiveness happened years later when he encountered his brothers for the first time since they had betrayed him.

The famine not only struck Egypt; it also ravaged Canaan where Joseph's family lived. His father heard that there was grain in Egypt, so he sent ten of Joseph's eleven brothers to go there to buy grain.

And who oversaw distribution of the food? Joseph, their brother. At first, they did not recognize Joseph when they requested food from him. We don't know why. Perhaps he had changed a lot over the years.

But Joseph recognized them. Not only did Joseph

provide bread and other food to his brothers, but he arranged for his whole family to come to Egypt where he could provide for them.

Think about it– if not for Joseph, his family would have died from the famine. But God had chosen Joseph and his eleven brothers to be the fathers of the twelve tribes of Israel. They were the great-grandsons of Abraham, to whom God promised to create a nation to testify of God's covenant to all other nations on the earth. In his foreknowledge, God knew that a terrible famine would strike the land of Canaan. And He chose Joseph to be strategically positioned in Egypt so that he could provide for his family, and thus preserve His chosen nation, Israel, and fulfill His promise to Abraham.

It took a few months before Joseph identified himself to his brothers. Why did he wait? The Bible doesn't tell us why. Perhaps he needed that time to process his emotions.

> *And Joseph said to his brothers, "Please come near to me." So they came near. "I am Joseph your brother, whom you sold into Egypt. But now, do not therefore be grieved or angry with yourselves because you sold me here; for God sent me before you to preserve life...And God sent me before you to preserve a posterity for you in the earth, and to save your lives by a great deliverance. So now it was not you who sent me here, but God; and He has made me a father to Pharaoh, and lord of all his house, and a ruler throughout all the land of Egypt."*[126]

Then Joseph instructed his brothers to go to Canaan and bring their father and brother Benjamin with them to Egypt, assuring them he would provide for their households.

Later, after their father died, Joseph's brothers worried that he would take revenge against them for the way they betrayed him years earlier. So they sent messengers to Joseph, falsely claiming that before he died, their father said he wanted Joseph to forgive his brothers for what they did to them.

> *"Now, please, forgive the trespass of the servants of the God of your father." And Joseph wept when they spoke to him. Then his brothers also went and fell down before his face, and they said, "Behold, we are your servants."*
>
> *Joseph said to them, "Do not be afraid, for am I in the place of God? But as for you, you meant evil against me; but God meant it for good, in order to bring it about as it is this day, to save many people alive. Now therefore, do not be afraid; I will provide for you and your little ones." And he comforted them and spoke kindly to them.*[127]

Wow. That's forgiveness. That's grace. It is also a beautiful example of the redemptive purpose of God in working all the negative things that happened to Joseph for his good, for the good of his family, and for God's ultimate purpose for the Jewish race.

By this time, Joseph's faith, wisdom, and character had matured so much that he could see the bigger picture of God's redemptive purpose. He knew that it was God, not his brothers, who had sent him to Egypt and allowed him to experience the difficulties he endured.

Like Joseph, we will all face many tests and much adversity in our lives. During adversity, your character will either grow or shrink. Stress and pressure will make you more patient, or less patient. You will become kinder, or more selfish. You will become more flexible and forgiving, or more hard and bitter. Your faith will become weaker, or stronger.

One thing that will not happen? You will not remain the same. Your character *will* change, for better or for worse, during seasons of adversity.

How should we respond to adversity? Faith untested is immature faith. The bigger your dream and its potential to expand the kingdom of God – the more faith, integrity, and godly character you need to steward the dream in a way that will not hurt you or others, and most importantly, will glorify God.

Resilient faith does develop in a life that is easy and free of stress, obstacles, trials, and pain. It grows as we learn to respond in a godly way to adversity.

Take responsibility for your attitudes. I like something John Maxwell says: “The greatest day in your life and mine is when we take total responsibility for our attitudes. That's the day we truly grow up.”

How do we pass the test of adversity? By choosing to appropriate God’s empowering grace to conduct ourselves with integrity, humility, and honour, no matter what is happening in our lives. By refusing bitterness. By making daily choices to trust God and obey His word. By refusing to compromise our character and biblical standards.

With each choice and act of obedience to God and His word, your character matures. Your faith grows. Each choice to keep your heart attitudes right, no matter what happens to you, takes you one more step along the pathway of purpose that God designed for you here on earth, and prepares you for your ultimate purpose in heaven.

Trials are not detours from destiny—they are the very tools God uses to shape us into vessels of His glory. It is through these very trials that our character is forged and our calling fortified. If we learn to trust God during those seasons – and it is a learning process – we will come to the other end with more resilient faith.

God doesn't waste pain; He uses it to prepare us for the purpose we were born to fulfill. As we surrender to the process, we begin to see that every challenge was a step toward the divine dreams He authored for us. Let the trials and tests remind you: you are being prepared for something greater than you can imagine!

The most difficult thing is the decision to act,
the rest is merely tenacity. – Amelia Earhart

CHAPTER FOURTEEN
USE IT OR LOSE IT

Ask any child what they would like to be when they grow up, and chances are that one of the things on his or her list will be: *astronaut*. It seems many adults hold on to that childhood dream, because every time NASA (the North American Space Agency) announces it will be hiring, they are flooded with applications. In one round of hiring, they received over eighteen thousand applications for just eleven spots.

You may have seen news reports about the billionaire space race between Jeff Bezos with his *Blue Origin*, Richard Branson with his *Virgin Galactic*, and Elon Musk with his *SpaceX*. All three spent billions of dollars on their rockets and charge $600 thousand plus for a one-day flight and up to $30 million for three or more days.

After all, flying in space looks so exciting and glamorous, doesn't it? You've probably seen news clips of astronauts floating around in their space capsules or on the International Space Station, or maybe you've seen movies like Apollo 13, Gravity, or Star Wars.

But as exciting and glamorous as it may seem to travel in space, it takes a terrible toll on the astronaut's bodies. We have all heard the cliché, *use it or lose it*. It's a cliché because it's true. It's a law of nature. Some call it the law of use. Whatever you want to call it, the principle is this: When something has not been used for a while, it atrophies. In other words, it weakens and wastes away.

That's a problem that has challenged NASA scientists for decades. Why? It's because our bodies need the resistance of gravity. When you don't have to counteract gravity, your muscles and bones lose strength.

Studies of astronauts who spent six months at the International Space Station found that their muscles lost more than 40 percent of their capacity for physical work. And no matter how good their shape was in before the astronauts left for the space station, they returned to earth with muscle tone that resembled that of the average 80-year-old. Once they return home, the astronauts invest a considerable amount of work, time, and exercise to rebuild their muscles and strength.

The Law of Use

It was the Greek physician Hippocrates, still today referred to as the Father of Medicine, who once said, "That which is used, develops. That which is not used, wastes away."

Use it or lose it. It applies to our bodies and our brains. And it also applies to our talents, spiritual gifts, and calling. The lack of use causes spiritual atrophy.

Jesus told several parables about the consequences of using or not using what we have received. One of those is the familiar parable of the five talents in Matthew chapter twenty-five. A master entrusted differing amounts of wealth, called "talents", to three individuals to manage while he went away on a long journey. A talent was a large monetary measurement equal to 6,000 denarii, which were the Greek and Roman silver coins. One denarius was considered a fair wage for one day of manual labor. That means a person would have to work 6,000 days to earn one talent. As you can see, a person who owned just one talent would be considered rich.

The owner gave one talent to one man, five talents to another, and ten to a third – the Bible says, "each according to his own ability."

One day the owner returned and asked each man to give an account of what he had done with the money. The two individuals who received five talents and two talents invested the money and doubled its value. The owner commended them and said the same thing to both:

> *"Well done, good and faithful servant; you were faithful over a few things, I will make you ruler over many things. Enter into the joy of your lord."*[128]

The third man in the parable didn't do so well. He admitted that he had hidden his talent in the ground. Why? He said, "I was afraid, and went and hid your talent in the ground."[129]

Why was he afraid? Perhaps he compared himself with the people who received more talents and buried his out of intimidation or envy. Perhaps he feared that he would fail and look foolish in the eyes of others. We know he did not trust the character of the owner, as he called him a "hard man."

Whatever the reasons, we know that God does not accept fear as an excuse for not using what we have received. The owner, who represents God in the parable, called this man a wicked and lazy servant. And he said, "So take the talent from him, and give it to him who has ten talents." Then Jesus went on to say,

> *"For to everyone who has, more will be given, and he will have abundance; but from him who does not have, even what he has will be taken away."*[130]

That may not seem fair. But what the third man in the parable lacked more than anything was a sense of accountability to the owner. God is never disappointed when we prayerfully do our best and fail. What grieves the heart of God is when we don't even try.

Whether you have one, five, or one hundred talents is not important. What is important is that you use what you have. We do not own our gifts, talents, skills, time, money, homes, bodies, or even our children, for that matter. God is the owner. We are stewards. And the way we steward what God has entrusted to us will determine if He entrusts us with more.

Can you see the wonderful promise in this parable? It is the promise of miraculous multiplication. When we are faithful to develop and use to the best of our ability whatever God has given us, He gives us more. He increases the effectiveness of our skills and gifts and multiplies his anointing, influence, and favour.

What is in your hand?

Throughout the Bible, God had a wonderful habit of using whatever a person possessed if they would simply surrender it to Him. He loves to use ordinary people to demonstrate His extraordinary power.

Moses

Take Moses for example. In Exodus chapter three, God appeared to Moses in a burning bush and told him that He wanted Moses to lead the children of Israel out of slavery in Egypt. At this point, Moses was an 80-year-old shepherd who had spent the past forty years tending flocks for his father-in-law.

God said: "Come now, therefore, and I will send you to Pharaoh that you may bring My people, the children of Israel, out of Egypt."[131]

How did Moses respond? With a series of excuses and reasons about why he was inadequate to do what God was asking him to do. For example, Moses said, "Who am I that I should go to Pharaoh, and that I should bring the children of Israel out of Egypt?" [132]

God assured Moses that he would not be alone. He said, "I will certainly be with you."[133] Then God gave Moses detailed instructions about what he was to say and do. Once again Moses expressed doubt. He said to God, "But suppose they will not believe me or listen to my voice; suppose they say, 'The Lord has not appeared to you.'[134]

How did God respond to that negative comment? He asked Moses a simple question:
"What is that in your hand?" Moses said, "A rod."[135] There was nothing special about the rod. It was a simple shepherd's staff that Moses had been using for forty years as he tended the flocks for his father-in-law.

God said, "Cast it on the ground."

As Moses cast it on the ground, it became a serpent and Moses fled from it. Then the Lord said to Moses, "Reach out your hand and take it by the tail" (and he reached out his hand and caught it, and it became a rod in his hand), "that they may believe that the Lord God of their fathers, the God of Abraham, the God of Isaac, and the God of Jacob, has appeared to you."[136]

Those of you familiar with the story will remember that God used Moses' staff for far more than turning it into a snake. God used this plain wooden staff to unleash all the plagues on Egypt to pressure Pharoah to let the Israelites go. When Pharoah finally let them go, God used that same staff in Moses' hand to part the Red Sea so the Israelites could pass. And once they had passed, God used that staff to cause the waters to come back and drown Pharoah's armies when they tried to chase after the Israelites.

There was nothing special about Moses' staff. It was an old, scratched-up piece of wood. But as Moses used it in obedience to God, the staff became a powerful tool for accomplishing divine purpose.

Do you feel like you are too old to serve God? Moses was eighty years old when God called him to lead the Israelites out of slavery in Egypt. Do you feel like you are too young? David was about fifteen years old when Samuel anointed him as king (although he was thirty years old when he became king). And young Timothy must have struggled with feelings of inadequacy about his age, because the apostle Paul exhorted Timothy to not despise his youth or consider it a hindrance to ministry.

Age, doubts, and feelings of inadequacy are immaterial. What matters is the call of God and His power and provision to take what you surrender to Him and use it for His glory.

David

Then there's David, when he faced the giant Goliath. In chapter eleven, we looked at how David overcame fear because of his zeal for God. Despite the fact David was not a soldier and had never been trained in warfare, he stepped out with courage and confidence, trusting in the power and faithfulness of his God.

What did he use to fight Goliath? He used what he knew. He used what was in his hand. David refused Saul's offer of armor and weapons, and instead used a sling and stones, the very tools he used in his everyday life as a shepherd protecting his sheep from predators. The sling and stones were pathetically inadequate compared to the armor and weaponry of the giant Goliath.

Not surprisingly, when David went out to battle Goliath, the giant laughed at him. But David's trust was not in the simplicity of his weapons; his trust was in the power and purpose of his God. And as David released a stone from the sling, it killed Goliath and gave the Israeli army victory over the Philistines.

Do you feel that what you have is too insignificant or ordinary? Do you hold back because you feel inadequate? Tell that to David. Your slingshot – whatever that may represent to you – will, in the hands of God, defeat giants and glorify your Lord.

The Poor Widow

Another example of God using what we have seen in the story of a poor widow. Elijah the prophet had run out of food, and the Lord told him to go to a city called Zarephath and find a widow woman who would feed him. So Elijah went and asked her for bread. But she explained her hopeless situation.

So she said, "As the Lord your God lives, I do not have bread, only a handful of flour in a bin, and a little oil in a jar; and see, I am gathering a couple of sticks that I may go in and prepare it for myself and my son, that we may eat it, and die."[137]

How did Elijah respond? He had the audacity to ask her to make him a cake first and then feed herself and her son. But he also promised that if she would do this, God would miraculously provide.

The poor widow chose to believe the words of the prophet. She risked the lives of herself and her son to give all that she had in her hand, though it was so little. What was the result? God multiplied her little to provide miraculously not just for their immediate needs, but for the future as well.

So she went away and did according to the word of Elijah; and she and he and her household ate for many days. The bin of flour was not used up, nor did the jar of oil run dry, according to the word of the Lord which He spoke by Elijah.[138]

Mary

Imagine being a 15-year-old girl living in a culture where pregnancy outside of marriage was a shameful scandal, and you receive a message from an angel that you would become impregnated by the Holy Spirit.

Typically, an unmarried woman who became pregnant in Mary's culture would suffer public shunning and disgrace. She would not only risk being ostracized by her family, friends, and synagogue – she risked losing Joseph and the dreams she had for their future. Mary was engaged to Joseph, and following the law, Joseph could cancel their betrothal contract by accusing her of sexual immorality. The truth of the matter is that she would risk her very life, as the penalty for adultery was stoning.

No wonder the scripture says, "Mary was greatly troubled at his word." What an understatement!

As an unmarried young woman from Nazareth, Mary had a very low social status. She was uneducated. She was not wealthy. She was just an ordinary girl. Did she feel inadequate and insufficient for the high calling of being the mother of the Son of God? I can't help but think she must have felt inferior to be chosen for such an honoured role.

But the angel Gabriel told Mary she was highly favoured by God. "Rejoice, highly favored one, the Lord is with you; blessed are you among women!"[139]

Mary knew her *yes* to the Lord posed many risks. Yet she bravely accepted her call when she said, "Behold the maidservant of the Lord! Let it be to me according to your word."[140]

Mary had no special talents, status, or resources. But she loved God and had found favour with Him. I love these words that she spoke while visiting her cousin Elizabeth:

My soul magnifies the Lord,
And my spirit has rejoiced in God my Savior.
For He has regarded the lowly state of His maidservant;
For behold, henceforth all generations will call me blessed.
For He who is mighty has done great things for me,
And holy is His name.[141]

What did Mary have to offer? Her "*yes*", her faith, and her obedience. And through the power of God, she fulfilled the amazing calling to be the mother of Jesus, the Son of God, Savior of the world!

A Few Loaves and Fish

My all-time favourite story of God empowering what we surrender to Him is when He miraculously multiplied a few loaves and fish to feed thousands of hungry people.

Jesus had been ministering all day long to a massive crowd of people. The Bible says there were five thousand men. Theologians estimate that when you include the women and children, there were likely between fifteen and twenty thousand people. Late in the day, the disciples became concerned about the large crowd and lack of food and nearby lodging, so they presented Jesus with a practical and logical solution to the problem.

When it was evening, His disciples came to Him, saying, "This is a deserted place, and the hour is already late. Send the multitudes away, that they may go into the villages and buy themselves food."[142]

What did Jesus think about their proposition? Apparently not much, for He said, "They do not need to go away. **You** give them something to eat."[143]

I can't help but wonder what the disciples were

thinking at that point. Were they thinking: *What is wrong with Jesus? Has He been out in the sun too long? How in the world are we supposed to feed this massive crowd?*

So they said to Him, "We have here only five loaves and two fish."[144]

What did Jesus say? Did He agree it would never be enough? Did he cast the loaves and fish aside, since they were so pathetically inadequate to feed such a large crowd? No. He said, "Bring them to Me."[145]

Jesus took those few supplies, the fives loaves and two fish, offered them up to heaven, thanked God for them, and blessed and broke them. Then He told the disciples to distribute them to the people. And you know the end of the story. Not only did everyone eat as much as they wanted, but the disciples also gathered twelve baskets of leftover fragments.

Remember – although the multiplication of the loaves and fish was truly an astounding miracle, it was not about God creating something out of nothing. Jesus took what they had – the few loaves and two fish – and multiplied them so there was more than enough to feed the massive crowd.

What do you have to offer to God? Your inner critic, or other people, or the devil will tell you that your gift is insignificant. And truth be told, it will be insignificant if you try to use it in your own strength, or if you don't use it at all.

The lesson behind these stories is not about Moses's rod, David's sling, the widow's handful of flour, Mary's youth and low social status, or a few loaves and fish. It is not about what you have, or what you don't have.

It is about our powerful, faithful God who can use and multiply whatever you have if you will simply give it to Him and use it to serve Him.

It was only as Moses stretched out his hand, David released the stones from his sling, the widow fed the prophet, Mary said *yes* to a shocking proposition, and a little boy willingly gave up his lunch of loaves and fish – that God's power was manifest.

I could make a long list of what I don't have, and I'm sure you could do the same.

> *But we have this treasure in earthen vessels, that the excellence of the power may be of God and not of us.*[146]

Friends, it is not about you or me appearing strong or powerful or sufficient. It's all about God. His strength, grace, and power are glorified in weak, insufficient, earthen vessels.

It is not what we have, or don't have, that makes the difference. It's the blessing of God on what we have. It's the size of our God, not the size of our gift. It's the strength of our God, not our own strength. It's the power of our God. As God spoke through the prophet to Zerubbabel: "Not by might nor by power, but by My Spirit." [147]

Again, what do you have? Does it seem small? Does it seem inadequate and insignificant compared to the size of your dream or compared to the gifts and achievements of others you know?

Whatever is in your hand– however small it may seem – if you are faithful to develop and use it, God will infuse it with His anointing, and He will entrust you with more.

God isn't asking you for what you don't have. He is asking you to thank Him for what you have, surrender it to Him, ask Him to bless it, and then by faith use it to serve others.

As you do that, He will infuse you and your gift with His power to expand the kingdom of God for His glory.

Today, take one step

"You don't have to be great to start," said the late best-selling author and motivational speaker Zig Ziglar. "But you have to start to be great."

You'll remember that we talked about developing an action plan in chapter eleven. How is that going? Are you still tweaking the plan? Do you find yourself revising your plan, again and again? Is it possible those constant revisions are an excuse to not step out in faith and act?

Once you have a plan, it's time to move. Your plan doesn't need to be perfect. Far from it. As you execute your plan, you will learn and change and grow. Some things will work; some won't. Life happens, circumstances change, and when necessary, you will adjust your plan.

You can only plan according to the spiritual revelation you have received at this point on your faith journey. As you grow in your relationship with God and take steps of faith as God directs, your revelation of God's purpose will expand.

On the other hand, if you avoid acting because you are continually revising and changing and perfecting your plan, you could easily get stuck in the *paralysis of analysis* – a phrase that originates in a children's story: *The Fox and the Cat.*

In the story, the fox and the cat were discussing what they would do if they were attacked by hounds. "I have a whole bag of tricks," boasted the fox, "which contains a hundred ways of escaping my enemies." In turn, the cat said, "I have only one, but I can generally manage with that."

Just at that moment, they heard the cry of a pack of hounds coming towards them. Immediately, the cat scampered up a tree and hid herself in the branches. "This is my plan," said the cat. "What are you going to do?"

The fox thought first of one way, then of another, and still another. While he continued debating his options, the hounds came nearer and nearer, and at last the fox in his confusion was caught by the hounds and killed.

Looking sad, the cat said: "Better one safe way than a hundred on which you cannot reckon."[148]

If your goal is to create a perfect, fail-safe plan, you'll never get anything done. People who wait to take action until every real or imagined obstacle is removed will never get beyond the starting gate. Many of the world's greatest geniuses died without having ever succeeded at anything. Why? It takes more than good intentions and talent to be successful. It takes boldness, faith, and obedience to God. Translated into everyday living, that means action.

So, take one step today. Tomorrow, take another. Keep saying *yes* to God. And keep taking one step after another to steward what God has given you.

Remember, big dreams come to life when we create small achievable goals that we act on – now!

What is one action step you can do today? Get started with just one thing. Then tomorrow ask yourself the same question. Each small step will help create a momentum that will propel you forward on your pathway of purpose.

Final Words

Dreams don't rise because we finally feel sufficient; they rise because God is. The world is still noisy with loss, delay, and doubt, but none of that cancels His calling or rewrites His promise: *"With God all things are possible."*

Perhaps a part of you once felt buried—delayed by disappointments, dulled by fear, weighed down by what-ifs. Yet even here, grace finds you. God has not changed. His purposes have not dimmed. He still invites you to place your everyday life in His hands and watch Him do what only He can do.

Again and again, scripture shows us that God uses the ordinary, the small, and the seemingly insignificant when placed in His hands: a shepherd's rod, a boy's sling, a widow's handful of flour, Mary's trembling yes, five loaves and two fish. None of them looked like enough. But all of them became more than enough in the hands of a faithful God.

The same is true for you. Perhaps you feel like your gifts are too small compared to the task ahead. Yet God is not asking you for what you don't have. He is asking you to offer what you do have—to thank Him for it, surrender it to Him, and take the next faithful step.

So breathe. Ask again. Listen again. This is your moment to dream again—not as nostalgia for what used to be, but in partnership with God's greater purpose now. Not because circumstances are easy, but because Christ is faithful.

Don't wait for perfect conditions or flawless plans. Don't compare your calling to another's. Begin with the next right step—one act of obedience, one conversation, one prayer, one risk of love. In God's economy, small seeds become harvests; simple offerings become signs of the Kingdom.

God has written you into His greater dream – the redemption of a hurting world. He calls you to be His hands, His voice, His heart, in your unique sphere of influence. You may never know this side of eternity how far the ripple effects of your obedience will reach. But heaven will reveal the lives touched because you chose to dream again, to act again, to believe again.

May you discover, as you move and act by faith, that God's dream for healing and redemption is nearer than you imagined—and that your unique part in it is both beautiful and essential.

When you look back, you'll see the pattern: not by might, not by power, but by His Spirit. May your life become living proof that with God, the small you give becomes more than enough—and that every God-breathed dream awakens as you use what's in your hand.

Twenty years from now you will be more disappointed by the things you didn't do than by the ones you did. So throw off the bowlines. Sail away from the safe harbor. Catch the trade winds in your sails. Explore. Dream. Discover."

–Mark Twain

ABOUT THE AUTHOR

Judy Rushfeldt is an award-winning author, international speaker, and leader whose mission is to inspire and equip others to live with wholeness, purpose, and joy.

She has been writing professionally for over 40 years, including authoring four books and writing hundreds of articles published in both faith-based and secular magazines. Her book, *Making Your Dreams Your Destiny*, won two national awards.

Judy's passion is to inspire others to step out of their comfort zones and cultivate the courage, character and faith necessary to discover and fulfill their God-ordained purpose and potential.

To contact Judy, and to see her other books and resources, visit:

JudyRushfeldt.com

NOTES

---

[1]CHAPTER 1

Scott Mendelson, "The Key Reason Audiences Love Tom Cruise," *Forbes*, August 30, 2018, https://www.forbes.com/sites/scottmendelson/2018/08/30/box-office-tom-cruise-mission-impossible-fallout-china/?sh=151ac1b7e0f8

[2] Dan. 11:32

[3] Matt. 19:26

[4] Isa. 43:16, 18-19

[5] Phil. 3:12b-14

[6] Heb. 11:6

[7] John 10:10

[8] John 12:46

[9] John 6:38

[10] Mark 10:45

[11] Luke 19:10

[12] Luke 4:18-19

[13] Eph. 2:10 AMPC

CHAPTER 2

[14] Ps. 139:13-16 NIV

[15] Rom. 8:28

[16] 2 Cor. 12:9

[17] Christine Caine, *Propel Women,* Retrieved February 13, 2025, https://www.propelwomen.org/content/interview-with-christine-caine/gjeb49

[18] Christine Caine, *Undaunted: Daring to do what God calls you to do*, (Zondervan, 2019), p.28

[19] Rom. 11:29

[20] John 3:3

[21] John 3:5-6

[22] Stephen Mansfield, *Never Give In: The Extraordinary Character of Winston Churchill*, (Turner Publishing Company, 1997), p. 39

[23] Ibid. pg. 14

CHAPTER 3

[24] John 16:13

[25] Prov. 29:18

[26] George Barna, *The Power of Vision*, (Regal Books, 1992) p. 71-72

[27] Isa. 55:8-9

[28] Eph. 1:17-18

[29] Ps. 119:105

[30] Heb. 4:12

[31] 1 Kings 19:12

[32] John 10:27

[33] Acts 13:2

[34] Prov: 20:27, Rom. 8:16

[35] James 3:17

[36] Prov. 11:14

[37] Acts 16:6-8

CHAPTER 4

[38] Ps. 119:105

[39] ibid

[40] Gen.12:1

[41] Heb. 11:8

[42] Dr. George Hill and Dr. Hazel Hill, *Adventure, Romance & Revival*, (Victory International Publishing, 1999)

CHAPTER 5

[43] NASA https://www.nasa.gov/news/

[44] Phil. 2:13 AMPC

[45] John 15:7-8

[46] Ps.32:8

[47] Laurie Beth Jones, *The Path: Creating your Mission Statement for Work and Life*, (Hachette Books, 2001) Section: Forming a Sense of Mission, Kindle.

[48] Daniel Coleman , "Pondering the Riddle of Creativity," *The New York Times*, March 22, 1992 https://www.nytimes.com/1992/03/22/movies/pondering-the-riddle-of-creativity.html

CHAPTER 6

[49] Peter Bregman, "Commentary: Why we are fascinated by Susan Boyle," *CNN.* April 22, 2009 https://edition.cnn.com/2009/SHOWBIZ/Music/04/22/bregman.boyle/index.html

[50] John Ortberg, *If you want to Walk on Water You've Got to Get out of the Boat*, (Zondervan, 2001), p. 58.

[51] Eph. 4:11-13

[52] 1 Cor. 12:11

[53] Rom. 12:4-8

[54] 2 Tim. 1:6-7

[55] 1 Pet. 4:10-11

CHAPTER 7

[56] Prov. 20:5 NIV

[57] Col. 3:17

[58] Rom. 8:28

[59]Nick Vujicic, Sermon, New Hope Church, Oahu, Hawaii, March 30, 2014, captured March 01, 2024. https://newhopeoahu.com/sermon/notes.php?id=W1413

[60] Nick Vujicic, "God's Miraculous Plan," posted May 13, 2013 by NickV Ministries, YouTube, 5:37, https://www.youtube.com/watch?v=SYuVx2LU5QM

[61] 2 Cor. 12:13-14

[62] Judg. 6:15-16

[63] Rom. 8:28

[64] 2 Cor. 1:3-5

[65] Isa. 55:8-11

CHAPTER 8

[66] 1 Pe. 4:10 NIV

[67] Isa. 55:8-11

[68] Ps. 32:8

CHAPTER 9

[69] Hab. 2:10

[70] John 16:13, Ps. 32:8

[71]

CHAPTER 10

Jim Korkis, *The Unofficial Walt Disney World 1971 Companion*, (Theme Park Press, 2019), p.3

[72] George Barna, *The Power of Vision*, (Regal Books, 1992) p. 71

[73] Mark 10:27

CHAPTER 11

[74] Stephen R. Covey, *How to Develop your Personal Mission Statement*, (Brilliance Publishing, 2013), chap 1, Kindle.

[75] Prov. 16:9

[76] Jack Canfield, Mark Victor Hansen, Les Hewitt, *The Power of Focus*, (Health Communications Inc., 2000) p.61-62

[77] Phil. 3:12-14

[78] Dr. Henry Townsend, *Necessary Endings*, (HarperCollins Publishers, 2010), p. 16

CHAPTER 12

[79] Heb. 6:11-12

[80] 1 Tim. 6:12

[81] 2 Tim. 4:7

[82] Eph. 3:17-19

[83] 1 Sam. 17:8-10

[84] 1 Sam. 17: 26 NIV

[85] v .29

[86] v .37

[87] 1 Sam. 17:45-47

[88] James 2:17 AMPC

[89] v .21-22

[90] Heb. 4:12 AMPC

[91] Ps. 119:89-90

[92] Matt. 7:24-27

[93] Josh. 1:3

[94] 2 Cor. 10:12

[95] Gal. 6:4-5 NLT

[96] David Bayles and Ted Orland, *Art & Fear: Observations on the Perils (and Rewards) of Artmaking*, (Capra Press, 1994), p 29

[97] Prov. 29:25

[98] Prov. 14:26-27

[99] Heb. 12:1

[100] 2 Tim. 4:7

CHAPTER 13

[101] 1 Pe. 6-7 ESV

[102] NavySeals.com, captured April 22, 2025, https://navyseals.com/nsw/hell-week-0/

[103] James 1:2-4 AMPC

[104] Prov. 17:3

[105] Luke.10:19

[106] Ps. 105:17-19

[107] Gen. 37:8

[108] Gen. 37:19-20

[109] Gen. 39:2-5

[110] Gen. 39:21-23

[111] Luke. 16:10,12

[112] Col. 3:23 NIV

[113] Gen. 39:7-8

[114] 1 Thess. 4:3-4

[115] Gen. 40:7-8

[116] Luke 10:36-37

[117] Gal. 4:23

[118] Gen. 17:17-18

[119] v. 19

[120] Gen. 18:14

[121] Gen. 41:14

[122] v. 15

[123] v. 16

[124] Gen. 41:33-36

[125] Gen. 41:39-41

[126] Gen. 45:4-5, 7-8

[127] Gen. 50:17-21

CHAPTER 14

[128] Matt. 25:21

[129] v. 25

[130] v. 29

[131] Exod. 3:10

[132] v.11

[133] v. 12

[134] Exod. 4:1

[135] v.2

[136] v.3-5

[137] 1 Kings 17:12

[138] v. 15-16

[139] Luke 1:21

[140] v. 38

[141] v. 46-49

[142] Matt. 14:15

[143] v.16

[144] v. 17

[145] v.18

[146] 2 Cor. 4:7

[147] Zech. 4:6

[148] Aesop, “The Fox and the Cat”. *Aesop's Fables* (Lit2Go Edition). Retrieved April 01, 2025, https://etc.usf.edu/lit2go/35/aesops-fables/393/the-fox-and-the-cat/

www.ingramcontent.com/pod-product-compliance
Lightning Source LLC
LaVergne TN
LVHW051502080426
835509LV00017B/1882
* 9 7 8 1 8 9 4 3 7 5 0 3 0 *